SALES PROMOTION ESSENTIALS

SALES
PROMOTION
ESSENTIALS

The 10 Basic Sales Promotion Techniques...And How To Use Them

DON E. SCHULTZ
WILLIAM A. ROBINSON
LISA A. PETRISON

Second Edition

NTC Business Books
a division of *NTC Publishing Group* • Lincolnwood, Illinois USA

Library of Congress Cataloging-in-Publication Data

Schultz, Don E.
    Sales promotion essentials / Don E. Schultz, William A. Robinson, Lisa Petrison.
—2nd ed.
      p.   cm.
    ISBN 0-8442-3366-8. — ISBN 0-8442-3367-6 (pbk.)
    1. Sales promotion. I. Robinson, William A., 1926– .
II. Title.
HF5438.5.S38 1992
658.8.2—dc20   91-45097
                                                     CIP

Published by NTC Business Books, a division of NTC Publishing Group
4255 West Touhy Avenue
Lincolnwood (Chicago), Illinois 60646-1975, U.S.A.

2 3 4 5 6 7 8 9 0 VP 9 8 7 6 5 4 3 2 1

Contents

Foreword

The field of sales promotion has been changing very rapidly. Today the emphasis is on strategic thinking and planning, and the marketer who effectively integrates sales promotion into the overall marketing mix has a distinct competitive advantage. Random couponing or price discounting without regard to such things as consumer behavior, product performance, advertising message, or competitive activity, simply shortchange the total marketing effort.

The authors of *Sales Promotion Essentials* are strong proponents of a fully integrated marketing strategy. The book discusses ten sales promotion tools available to accomplish short-term marketing objectives. It explains how each promotional technique works and under what circumstances the technique should be considered. But more than that, this book provides the strategic understanding and insight into when to use these various promotional devices to maximize the entire marketing plan.

In the past, business growth came fairly easy. When product and service businesses were in the early stages of their life cycles, virtually any kind of promotional activity brought a quick sales response. Now with more mature businesses, growth requires a much more sophisticated promotion plan. *Sales Promotion Essentials* provides a close-up look at the building blocks that form the tactical foundation of a promotion plan, as well as the strategic insight to provide full integration with other elements of the marketing mix.

Dennis Lahey
Director/Advertising & Promotion
Kimberly-Clark

Chapter One

What Is Sales Promotion and Why Has It Grown?

Sales promotion in the United States is a big, big business—and one that is continuing to grow significantly each year. In 1990, for example, U.S. marketers invested more than $125 billion in sales promotion—more than twice the $49 billion spent in 1980.

To get some idea of how important sales promotion has become to today's marketers, consider these facts:

- Sales promotion represents more than two-thirds of the marketing budget at most consumer products companies.

- In 1990, trade promotion represented 44 percent of marketers' total promotional budget, consumer promotion represented 25 percent, and media advertising represented 31 percent. (In 1980, 34 percent of expenditures were on trade promotion, 22 percent were on consumer promotion, and 44 percent were on media advertising.)

- More than 250 billion coupons (1,000 for every U.S. resident) were distributed in the United States in 1990, up from only 40 billion in 1975.

- In 1990, U.S. consumers saved $3.5 billion by redeeming 7 billion coupons.

- Marketers spent $27 billion in 1989 (a 7.1 percent increase from 1988) on various premiums, including sales and dealer incentives, through-the-mail premiums, continuity plans, sweepstakes and contests.[1]

---

[1]*Premium/Incentive Business.*

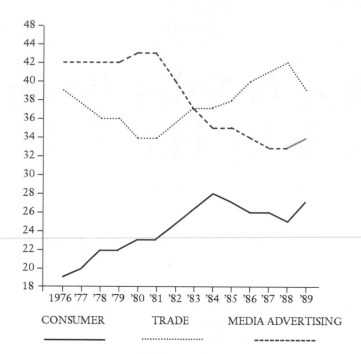

Exhibit 1.1. Change in Promotional Expenditures
Source: NCH Promotional Services.

Why Such Enormous Growth?

Obviously, sales promotion expenditures have become an increasingly important part of doing business in the United States. This tremendous growth can be attributed to a number of factors:

Sales promotion produces results. Dollar for dollar, marketers usually get more immediate "bang for their buck" with sales promotion than with any other marketing activity. Sending out a coupon, running a trade deal, or giving a rebate affects consumer and retailer behavior quickly, usually producing a big spike in sales as buyers rush to take advantage of the short-term deal. Most marketing managers have found that if they need a quick sales boost, sales promotion produces results.

Sales promotion results occur quickly. Communications tools such as advertising or public relations are usually perceived as an investment, with sales occurring at some undetermined point in the future. On the other hand, sales promotion usually works during a finite period of time, often showing results within days or even hours.

For many marketers who are under increased pressure from management and/or stockholders to get fast results, sales promotion can therefore be very attractive.

Sales promotion results are measurable. Because promotion results in such quick and strong sales, its effects are easy to observe and measure. Therefore sales promotion has generally been viewed as the most scientific tool in the marketing mix. It has been the subject of a large number of efficacy studies by researchers, who in some cases have been able to create formulas predicting exactly how different kinds and amounts of sales promotion will affect sales in different product categories.

Sales promotion is relatively easy and inexpensive to implement. Many marketers today are able to estimate, with a strong degree of accuracy, exactly what will happen to the sales of a brand, and to the sales of its competitors, based on the results of a particular promotion. This has in many cases made promotions easier to design and carry out, and it has allowed companies to move the design of sales promotion activities to lower levels in the management hierarchy (for instance, sales promotion is generally planned and often managed by assistant brand managers and by project-oriented promotion agencies). In addition, sales promotion may be less expensive than other forms of marketing communications. For instance, printing coupons, distributing them through free-standing inserts, and reimbursing the retailers who redeem them may often be a sizable expenditure. On a cost versus results basis, however, sales promotion may be much less expensive than producing and airing television commercials to reach the same audience, especially since the costs of mass media advertising have gone up substantially in recent years.

Why Sales Promotion Works

The main reason that the sales promotion area has grown so dramatically in recent years is because *sales promotion works*, especially in today's more competitive marketing environment. The apparent effectiveness of sales promotion programs has become more and more important in ensuring the success of a majority of products in the marketplace.

Other factors have also contributed to sales promotion's growth. Most product categories and successful brands in the United States are already mature, meaning that most products' sales increases must come mainly from stealing share from competitors' brands rather than from increasing the size of the category. Also, many categories are composed of parity brands, meaning that it can be difficult to find or create meaningful advertising that differentiates one product from another. Finally, growth in the U.S. economy has

Awareness
Information Gathering
Pre-purchase Evaluation
Decision Making
PURCHASE
Post-purchase Evaluation

Exhibit 1.2.   Stages of Consumer Decision Making

slowed, and consumers are often more price and promotion sensitive during periods of recession or slow growth.

Redefining Sales Promotion's Role

The traditional definition of sales promotion has been: *Sales promotion gives consumers a short-term incentive to purchase a product.* This definition is accurate, as far as it goes—coupons or value packs or trade deals or other promotions do give consumers more of a reason to purchase a product immediately, and most of these promotions do last for a reasonably short period of time. However, this definition does not state exactly why promotions work nor how they affect the brand from an overall strategic point of view.

To understand how promotions work, it is important to understand the consumer-buying process. Except in the case of very low-involvement, inexpensive, impulse items, most people do not make snap decisions about what products to buy. Instead, they go through a variety of consideration stages before reaching their final decision, including awareness, information gathering, pre-purchase evaluation, decision making, purchase, and post-purchase evaluation.

Different types of marketing activities often work in different ways to affect various aspects of this buying process. Advertising and public relations, for instance, generally affect the awareness, the information-gathering, and perhaps the evaluation stages for new products, as consumers learn about products and consider whether or not they might be worth buying. These types of promotions also provide reminders about established products, which may be at parity with other brands. Personal selling may also affect the information-gathering and decision-making stages of the buying process, as the salesperson works to relieve consumers' specific doubts about a product and provides extra encouragement to go ahead and make the purchase.

Sales promotion, however, generally works on a direct behavioral level. Generally, rather than influencing awareness or attitudes—which may or may not eventually translate into corresponding behavior—most types of sales promotion hit directly at the decision-making and purchasing stages of the buying process, meaning that while sales promotion usually has less long-term effectiveness, it has more immediate results. Sending consumers a coupon for a product they sometimes use, for example, may not change their overall opinion about that product, but it may cause them to purchase it when they ordinarily would not do so.

Sales promotion is able to change behavior directly because, in short, it alters the price/value relationship that the product offers the buyer. In some cases this means lowering the price, perhaps with a coupon or rebate or trade deal or on-package price discount. In other cases it means adding something of value to the product—for instance, giving consumers a related item in the package or through a mail-in offer, supplying them with more of the product, or offering them a chance to win a prize in a contest or sweepstakes.

Altering the price/value relationship means that consumers get a better deal and therefore have more of a reason to purchase the product. Moreover, because most promotions last for only a short period of time, consumers have a reason to purchase the product immediately, rather than waiting.

As stated, sales promotion has become increasingly important to U.S. manufacturers. However, although the amount of money that companies spend on sales promotion has grown dramatically, most marketers' overall approach to the field has remained basically the same as it was two decades ago.

Most companies today know that sales promotion is a good way to increase short-term sales and profits. Many sales promotions have become more complex in recent years, often incorporating a variety of promotional elements. In addition, as noted, many marketers and researchers are increasing their attempts to measure the results of sales promotion activities and to conduct them in a more scientific manner.

Nevertheless, the field of sales promotion has in general remained oriented to the short term. In addition, promotions are often not well related to the other strategic elements of the brand's marketing mix. Most of the research into sales promotion has centered on how particular promotions, and levels of promotion, affect short-term sales, not on how those promotions fit into the overall marketing mix and into the overall strategic focus of the company or brand.

As a result, sales promotion is often viewed as a simple, reactionary device in the war to increase immediate sales and profit. Many companies even view sales promotion as no more than a necessary evil—although marketers often wish they could get rid of their promotions or reduce their importance, a mixture of competitive pressures, consumer expectations, and desire for short-term profit often cause those managers to keep investing money in sales promotion.

In short, sales promotion has tended to be a tactically driven discipline. Marketing managers have typically used promotions as short-term volume boosters, often without much analytical thought.

What has generally been missing in the industry is a strategic focus, that is, an examination of how various sales promotion activities affect the overall short-term and long-term positions of the brand in the marketplace. Each category in the market has a different set of dynamics at work within it, and each brand within each category has its own strengths and weaknesses, its own unique positioning and reputation, and its own set of loyal or fickle customers. To be fully effective, sales promotion programs need to recognize all of these factors, and they should be developed in the context of everything else that's happening with a particular brand.

It is therefore appropriate to move to a more strategic definition, one that recognizes sales promotion's role in the overall brand-building process: *Sales promotions are marketing and communications activities that change the price/value relationship of a product or service perceived by the target, thereby (1) generating immediate sales and (2) altering long-term brand value.*

This definition recognizes that sales promotion motivates consumers to purchase a product immediately, either by lowering the price (with the use of coupons, trade discounts, or other means) or by adding value (for instance, with the use of sweepstakes or value packs).

In addition, the definition takes into consideration the concept of a target audience, implying that promotion should be aimed at a specific group of consumers rather than at the population at large. It also recognizes the role of sales promotion in the area of perceived value, suggesting that this is not always a simple matter of concrete attributes and actual price.

Most significantly, the new definition addresses the effect that sales promotion has on the long-term brand value (also known as the brand franchise). The brand franchise is important because it determines how likely consumers are to buy a particular product rather than one of its competitors' products, all else (such as price or distribution) being equal. A stronger brand franchise means that customers are less likely to be affected by competitive promotional activities. In addition, because it means that there is a consumer demand for the product, retailers are more likely to be willing to carry it and possibly to accept a lower margin on it.

Sales promotion does have a residual market value, that is, there may be a long-term effect on the brand franchise after the promotion is over. Sales promotion may also have an effect on the relationship value of the brand, that is, on how positively or negatively consumers feel about a particular product or company.

These types of long-term effects from sales promotion have usually been viewed as negative, with many people believing that too much promotion detracts from the long-term value of the brand. This problem has been particularly prevalent in certain consumer products categories, such as soft drinks or paper and plastic products, where frequent discounting has made the "real" price of the product unclear and has taught consumers and retailers to buy only on deal.

However, depending on the particular situation and goals, sales promotion may also have a positive long-term effect on the brand and on residual market value. The scope of this effect—and whether it occurs—depends on the individual situation, the particular promotion used, and the type of customer targeted.

The rest of this book is designed to help you plan sales promotion programs within a more strategic framework. It will examine the kinds of effects that various sales promotion activities have in different situations—in terms of affecting short-term sales before and immediately following the promotion, and in terms of the long-term value of the brand.

Chapter Two

Planning
Sales Promotion

Like any other type of marketing activity, sales promotion needs to be evaluated in the context of how it fits into the overall strategy for a particular brand. To be able to conduct promotion activities effectively, it is helpful for marketers to first answer the following questions:

1. *Who are the customers we want to reach?* It is an accepted tenet of marketing that not all customers are alike. In fact, a large percentage of traditional marketing activities is oriented toward segmenting consumers into relevant groups and then determining the appropriate messages to be used to target each group.

Most marketing activities segment consumers according to demographics, psychographics, and other permanent personal characteristics that are assumed to affect the kinds of products that these people are likely to need or desire. Awareness of these personal characteristics is useful in developing products, packaging, advertising, public relations, or other kinds of activities that affect consumer attitudes toward products. Such an awareness is essential to the evaluation of how useful those products are likely to be to them.

As was stated in Chapter 1, however, sales promotion usually works best in affecting behavior, not attitudes. Therefore it seems to make more sense with sales promotion to segment consumers according to their general *behavior*, that is, whether or not they buy the brand, or another product in the category, some or all of the time.

2. *What are the reasons for that behavior?* Just because two people act the same way doesn't necessarily mean that their reasons for doing so are the same. For instance, a person may leave a party early because he is bored, because he is shy, because he hates loud

music, because he has a headache, or because he has another engage-
ment. In order to persuade him to stay, it is necessary to understand
why he's leaving, not just to observe his behavior. We can then take
the appropriate action (give him an aspirin, turn down the stereo,
or simply let him leave).

The same principle applies to the field of sales promotion. Consumers may choose to purchase or not to purchase a product for a
wide variety of reasons. For instance, they may buy a particular
brand because they believe it is the best one on the market, because
it is less expensive than competitive products, because of habit, or
because of a combination of these factors.

It is important to analyze why consumers behave the way they
do, because this may affect whether—and by how much—they will
be influenced by a particular sales promotion program.

3. *What is the goal of the program?* Different sales promotion
programs are used for different reasons in order to achieve vastly
different ends. For instance, some promotions are designed to
achieve consumer trial, with the hope that triers will convert to future
buyers. Promotions may be used to match or preempt competitive
activities, in order to keep loyal customers from defecting to other
products. Some promotions are designed solely to create a short-term
sales spike, perhaps to meet the profitability goals of a certain period
of time. Obviously, there are many reasons why sales promotion is
used—and this needs to be considered in the planning process.

To tie these elements together, it is helpful to introduce a framework that segments consumers into different categories based on
their buying behavior.

One commonly used scheme is a segmentation framework developed by Professor Leigh McAlister (University of Texas, Austin).
This framework segments consumers of a product category according to whether they are brand loyal (generally using just one
brand) or switchers (alternating between two or more brands). According to the model, loyal customers may stockpile (that is, buy
products on deal and hoard them for future use) some or all of the
time, or they may be classified as not deal-prone. Switchers may also
be classified as not deal-prone (assumably interested in variety or in
meeting different needs with different products), or they may let
promotions affect their product choices, perhaps sometimes stockpiling product when they get a particularly good deal.

Used in a strategic analysis, the McAlister model can help promotion managers to better understand their customers. However, it
is a bit simplistic in that it assumes that consumers either are or are
not deal-prone. In reality, the dichotomy isn't nearly that complete.
Almost all consumers are sometimes influenced by some kind of

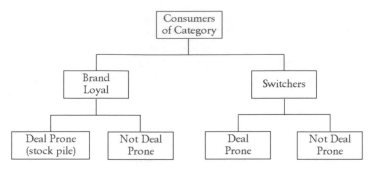

Exhibit 2.1. McAlister Segmentation Model

sales promotion. For instance, a woman who believes that clipping coupons is a waste of time may still purchase a product because of an on-package price reduction or a sweepstakes, and even the most ardent coupon clipper may sometimes buy an attractive product at a high price without a coupon.

Therefore, for the purpose of this book, it seems to make more sense to categorize consumers by their typical buying behaviors and by what appears to be causing those behaviors. It then becomes possible to choose appropriate promotional techniques that match the specific goals for the brand.

Based on their purchase behaviors, consumers can generally be divided into five categories: loyal users, competitive loyals, switchers, price buyers, and nonusers of the category.

Loyal Users

Loyal users are people who buy a particular brand on a more or less consistent basis. (The term *loyal user* has actually become a relative one in recent years, as fewer consumers have chosen to stick with just one brand. For instance, in some categories, such as toilet tissue, even the most loyal users may buy a particular brand only 60 percent of the time or less. For the purposes of this book, therefore, we will assume that a loyal user is someone who usually, but not necessarily always, buys a particular brand.)

When addressing a company's own loyals, the goal is not to change behavior but to reinforce it, thereby preventing defection and/or increasing current customers' consumption of the brand.

Reinforcing Existing Behavior

In very few cases are consumers unconditionally loyal to a particular product. Instead, they usually make the purchasing decisions they do because of a specific set of factors. They may honestly believe that "their" brand is the best one on the market, or they may think

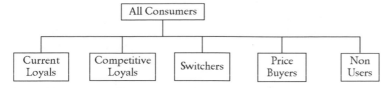

Exhibit 2.2.   New Segmentation Framework

that it's usually a good deal. Habit, or inertia, may also cause them to buy the same product over and over again.

An important point is that loyal consumers can sometimes be won over to competitive products with a change in price, the successful communication of product value, or the simple breaking of consumer habit. Companies may be wise, therefore, to take measures to hold onto their loyal customers with the judicious use of sales promotion programs.

Increased Usage

One good way to improve overall sales is to increase usage among current customers. Usually this is done by getting a customer to purchase a product when he or she would not ordinarily do so, or to purchase more of the product than usual in the expectation that the extra quantity will be readily consumed. Many consumers who buy an extra-large rather than a large bag of potato chips, for example, will find that the additional amount is easily consumed before the next week's shopping trip.

In other cases, sales promotion may result only in changes in purchase timing among brand loyals, who may take advantage of a good deal and then stockpile the product in the home for future use. A customer who notices bathroom tissue on sale, for instance, may purchase extra to have on hand but probably won't use any extra product just because it's in the house. Therefore future purchases by that customer will probably be curtailed. Changing purchase timing may be an appropriate end in and of itself for some sales promotion programs, however, depending on inventory and manufacturing constraints, the competitive situation, and the financial goals of the brand and the company.

Cross-Selling

Another way to capitalize on brand loyals—or, indeed, on anyone who ever purchases the product—is to attempt to sell them related products. For instance, a skin-care product manufacturer may attempt to sell cleanser to loyal users of its night creams. A doughnut shop may attempt to encourage customers to buy coffee with their regular pastry purchases. These kinds of cross-selling activities may be encouraged by certain types of sales promotion programs.

Competitive Loyals

Competitive loyals are people who use the product category and who usually buy a competitor's brand. We believe that there are three kinds of consumers who may be brand loyal: intense loyals, value buyers, and those constrained by habit.

Intense Loyals

Consumers may choose a brand because they believe it is the best one on the market, even if it is more expensive than the others. For instance, a woman may always use a certain brand of cosmetics because she thinks that those products are best for her skin. Even in mundane categories such as soft drinks, many consumers are loyal to either Coke or Pepsi, continuing to purchase their favorite even when the competitive brand is much less expensive.

Value Buyers

Consumers may be loyal to a particular brand because it appears to provide the most utility for the cost, even if it is not the best one on the market. For instance, if one dishwashing detergent is consistently priced much lower than competitive products but appears to be almost as good in terms of quality, then consumers may purchase it on a regular basis.

Brands may also acquire loyalty because they are of relatively good quality and are affordable. For instance, many consumers might concede that Mercedes is their preferred automobile and that the brand would be worth the cost—if they had the money available. If that isn't the case, they might then repeatedly purchase Toyota or another acceptable but more affordable brand.

Habit-Bound Buyers

Some consumers consistently purchase a brand not because they have made a conscientious study of its perceived value and price in comparison to that of other products on the market, but because it has become their habit to do so.

This type of mentality usually applies to relatively low-involvement products, and it may be more prevalent among consumers who are time-pressed, because it streamlines the buying process. Consumers who buy out of habit have created a simplified decision-making rule that eliminates the need for much thinking—for instance, "If we run out of laundry detergent, buy Tide."

One question here is how consumers originally went about choosing the brand that they now use out of what appears to be habit. Consumers may have started using a particular brand by chance, but they may also have begun using it because they felt that it was actually better than the other products on the market. These original reasons may be difficult to determine, but they may also be important in predicting how susceptible consumers are likely to be to sales promotion programs for other products.

Switchers

Switchers (or "swing users") are people who purchase a variety of brands within a product category. Switchers may be people who use a company's brands as well as competitive ones, or they may be people who only use other companies' products. However, those who switch only among competitive brands are also somewhat like competitive loyals in the way that they must be addressed, as both categories include people who for one reason or another don't currently use a particular brand and probably will be more difficult to convince of its merits.

As brand loyalty has decreased in recent years, the percentage of consumers who can be described as switchers has become a larger part of the population. Addressing switchers has, therefore, become an increasingly important aspect of sales promotion.

People who switch brands may do so for a variety of reasons, or for a combination of those reasons.

Availability

Sometimes people switch brands because their favorite product is not always available at the retail level and they are not willing to go out of their way to find it. For instance, even if a woman is brand loyal to Land O' Lakes margarine, she may not be willing to visit other retailers to find it if it is not carried at the store where she does most of her grocery shopping. Therefore even consumers who are intensely brand loyal may become switchers on certain occasions.

Obviously, availability is a distribution problem. Nevertheless, consumer and retailer promotions may both be used to combat the problem.

Value

Consumers may evaluate the price/value relationship for each brand, or for each product in a set of "acceptable" brands, on each shopping trip, choosing the brand that appears to be the best buy on that particular occasion. Because prices may vary from day to day or from store to store, consumers may buy different brands to fulfill the same need.

Even if consumers strongly prefer a certain brand, they may choose a competitive brand if the price is right. For instance, a person might like Aqua-Fresh toothpaste but may buy Close-Up instead if the price differential is more than 30 cents.

Occasion Usage

Sometimes a consumer may buy different brands within the same category to fulfill different needs or to be consumed on different usage occasions. One classic example of this is the beer drinker who buys Budweiser to consume during the week and Michelob to impress friends on the weekend. Other studies have shown that consumers may buy softer, decorative toilet tissue for holiday guests, then use the less expensive brands during the rest of the year.

If consumers consistently use the same brand for the same type of usage occasion, however, then they can basically be considered to be brand loyal to that product, since the dynamics are usually the same as with people who are completely brand loyal. To these types of people, it is almost as if there are two totally separate product categories, and they are brand loyal within those categories. They therefore should be addressed as such.

Variety

In some categories and with some consumers, variety is preferred for its own sake. This is a particularly big factor in the breakfast cereal category, where children or adults may tire of eating the same thing morning after morning and choose a variety of products and brands to relieve the monotony. This principle may also be in effect in other categories where many products prevail and where boredom can be a problem, including candy bars, cake mixes and—as people transfer their own desire for variety to their perception of what their cats and dogs want—pet food.

Price Buyers

Some consumers purchase brands solely on the basis of price. These customers may consistently purchase one brand if it is always the least expensive one in the marketplace, or they may switch among brands if some products vary in price across time. For instance, price buyers may consistently buy generic spaghetti sauce, unless one of the nationally advertised brands has a particularly good deal and matches the generic's price one week.

Price buyers generally either have little disposable income and can't afford to purchase the more expensive products or attach little importance to the differences between brands. For instance, some purchasers of flour believe that all brands are exactly the same, and therefore they always purchase the least expensive one. Most advertising and other image-building promotional techniques are designed to alter this view and make one brand appear to be more desirable than others, thereby removing the commodity image and increasing the price that consumers will be willing to pay for certain brands.

In most categories, price buyers tend to be a minor, but growing, percentage of the population. There is evidence that price buyers in a category are often heavy users of that category, however. The fact that they buy so much of the product may account for the reason that they are so price sensitive.

Nonusers

Nonusers are people who don't currently use any product in a particular category. Their failure to do so may be attributed to several factors.

Price

Some people would like to purchase a particular type of product but can't afford to do so. For instance, many people may wish they had their own helicopters to commute quickly back and forth from work, but they do not have enough money to make the investment.

Value

In some cases people don't buy a certain type of product because they believe it to be overpriced. For instance, some people refuse to buy convenience products like gourmet frozen dinners because they think they are too expensive and not worth the money.

Lack of Need

In some cases consumers may believe that the use of a particular product will not improve their lives, or they may in fact have absolutely no need for that product. For instance, some people don't use mouthwash because they don't think they need it. People without young children obviously have no reason to purchase diapers or baby car seats, no matter how attractive a deal they get on them.

In summary, consumers may behave in different ways for widely divergent reasons. Although these categorizations of usual buying behaviors may appear to be a little obvious, they can be helpful in segmenting consumers for the development of various kinds of sales promotion programs.

Incidentally, none of these classifications should be considered absolute. In many categories, consumers may move in and out of different classifications, perhaps moving from brand loyalty to a particular product to becoming a switcher to dropping out of the category. However, what is important is not the behavior of any individual consumer, but the general tendencies of the population as a whole. These can be gauged by marketers through a wide variety of research techniques.

Once marketers understand the dynamics occurring in a particular category at a specific point in time, they can then choose the appropriate promotional programs to best contribute to the specific goals they want to achieve.

Chapter Three

Selecting the Proper Promotional Tools

Once marketers understand the dynamics occurring within their product category and have determined the particular consumers and consumer behaviors they want to influence, they can then go about using various promotional techniques to achieve those goals.

As the promotional techniques are discussed, it is important to realize that each can produce impressive immediate results in most categories and for most brands. This is the way that many marketers view promotional tools—as a sure way to achieve a certain amount of sales over a particular period in time.

However, it is also important to realize that not all promotions affect all customers in the same way. In fact, certain sales promotions that are extremely effective at changing the behavior of one type of consumer may do nothing to affect another type. Before conducting promotional programs, therefore, it is crucial that marketers take a hard look at the dynamics currently occurring in the category, including the percentage of the population that engages in each of the purchase behaviors, the reasons for those behaviors, and the changes that are currently occurring in the marketplace. After they determine the general characteristics of the population and after they decide which of these consumer groups they want to influence and what their goals are, the marketers can then go about designing the promotional programs that will best help them to reach those goals.

This chapter covers some broad principles concerning which kinds of sales promotions are appropriate to effectively target different kinds of consumers. Each of these techniques is described more thoroughly in the rest of the book; the discussion here is intended to tie them together and show some of the alternative ways that different consumers can be approached. This chapter also covers the

Exhibit 3.1.   Types of Consumers and Sales Promotion Results Desired

Type	Description	Desired Results
Current Loyals	People who buy the "right" product most or all of the time.	Reinforce behavior, increase consumption, change purchase timing.
Competitive Loyals	People who buy a competitors' product most or all of the time.	Break loyalty, persuade to switch to promoted brand.
Switchers	People who buy a variety of products in the category.	Persuade them to buy the "right" brand more often.
Price Buyers	People who consistently buy the least expensive brand.	Appeal to them with low prices or supply added value that makes price less important.
Nonusers	People who don't use any product in the category.	Create awareness of category and product, persuade them that product is worth buying.

effects that some promotions can have on long-term sales and on the brand franchise.

Consumer Segments and Sales Promotion Techniques

The various consumer segments described in Chapter 2 generally react differently to different sales promotion techniques.

Loyal Users

When companies look at consumers who are more or less loyal to their brands (*loyal* meaning that they purchase the desired product a large percentage of or all of the time and have relatively positive feelings toward it), they will not want to *change behavior*. Rather, they need to reinforce that behavior, increase product usage, or expand upon current product usage.

Reinforcing Behavior

By reinforcing loyal customers' present behavior, companies attempt to prevent them from being lured away by competitors' promotional activities. In doing this, marketers find it helpful to give those consumers some extra reason to stick with the brand.

One way to accomplish this is through continuity programs. Since loyal customers intend to buy the brand in the future, they probably will be willing to sign up for continuity programs. Once signed up, they may be more resistant to the promotional efforts of other brands. "Extras" (such as bonus packs, sweepstakes, specialty packages, or premiums) may also serve to enhance the perceived value of the brand and make the consumer believe that it is a good choice.

Price promotions are of more limited value in reinforcing behavior. Loyals will certainly be willing to take advantage of coupons or discounts, but it is unlikely that these activities will increase their brand loyalty in the future; in fact, some studies show that too-frequent discounting may even hurt the image of the brand among loyal consumers. Nevertheless, some price promotions may be necessary in certain cases simply to counter competitive activities and prevent core users from being lured away to other products.

Increasing Usage

A good way to capitalize on current users of a brand is to persuade them to purchase additional product. This product may be immediately consumed or it may be stockpiled for future use. Which of these scenarios occurs depends on a variety of factors, such as the type of product being used, how much is already being consumed, and whether the product can replace others currently being used. Ice cream bars, for instance, may be consumed easily by consumers who want snacks, whereas toothpaste consumption may have no potential for increasing. On the basis of their experiences with the product, most managers can predict relatively easily how quickly the extra product sold to current customers will be used up.

In some cases, too, simply shifting purchasing timing to the present may be beneficial in and of itself. Sometimes this may help companies to meet the profitability or sales goals of a particular period in time; at other times getting consumers to purchase extra product will mean that they will be less likely to buy a competitive brand in the near future.

Most sales promotion techniques can, at least at times, be successful in persuading current customers to increase their purchases of products. Probably the most direct method is through bonus packs, which give consumers an incentive to stock up. Price promotions may be successful in getting people to buy more product than they ordinarily might buy; whether this results in overall increased volume over time depends, as stated, on the overall behavioral dynamics of the category.

Continuity plans also may result in increased purchases, as consumers strive to acquire enough "points" to obtain the desired reward. (This may not be an effective tool in some situations where the product is high-priced or infrequently needed, however. For instance, frequent flyer programs are unlikely to encourage most people to fly more, since the cost of each flight is so high. Instead, frequent flyer programs tend to work best in creating loyalty among travelers who would otherwise switch from airline to airline.)

Interest-generating promotions such as bonus packs, specialty packaging, premiums, and point-of-purchase materials may also succeed in selling additional product to current users. Sweepstakes or contests can also be extremely successful in certain circumstances, particularly when entry can be tied to product usage. For instance, McDonald's has experienced strong increased volume with its sweepstakes promotions, which require consumers to visit a restaurant to pick up a game piece.

Cross-Selling

Promotions may be used to sell additional, different products to current customers. For instance, coupons for other brands may be included in product packaging, or bonus packs may offer free samples of the secondary item. Two or more related items have also been tied together in sweepstakes, rebate, or premium offers.

Competitive Loyals

Competitive loyals are obviously a tough group to win over. In many cases, these consumers are particularly predisposed toward their current brand, and they may not be willing to consider other products. In addition, these people have undoubtedly been hit with promotions for competitive brands in the past, and they have been generally unaffected by them. It is therefore likely that most ordinary promotions will continue to be ineffective.

Intense Loyals

The conversion of competitive loyals is a particularly big problem with people who are truly convinced of a particular brand's merits and who are psychologically committed to that brand. For these people, it is almost as though other brands in the category do not even exist; they are therefore likely to be immune to sales promotion activities. One exception to this might be sampling, which could introduce some intense loyals to the superior qualities of a competitive product. This will produce sales, however, only when the sampled brand has not been tried before and when it is noticeably superior in some way to the one currently being used.

Value Seekers

Competitive loyals who believe that "their" brand is generally the best *buy* on the market (but not necessarily the best-quality product) are not quite as resistant to sales promotion as are intense loyals, but they are nevertheless likely to be tough sells. Probably the best tool, again, is sampling, but only for brands that have not yet been tried and that have some obvious advantage over the currently used brand. Other sales promotion tools—high-value coupons, attractive sweepstakes, specialty packaging, bonus packs—may also be somewhat effective in certain circumstances, depending on how much value they appear to bring to the brand and on the consumer's attitude toward the product being promoted. Perhaps the main problem here is simply getting loyal customers to notice and consider promotions for brands they don't use, since they usually do not pay attention to materials concerning other brands.

Habit-Bound Buyers

Getting consumers to notice the promotion is also a key issue when inertia is a problem; however, once these consumers who buy from habit do notice the competitive brand, making a sale may be much easier than with other loyals. Sampling may be particularly effective in persuading consumers who buy out of habit, providing that the quality of the brand being promoted is superior and noticeable. Other promotions that create consumer interest may also be useful, including sweepstakes, bonus packs, specialty packaging, and premiums. What usually do not work are price promotions, as inertia buyers usually aren't even looking at price, although a particularly high-value coupon may catch the attention of a few of these consumers.

It is worth noting that in the case of consumers who are currently brand loyal because of inertia, the method of promotion delivery may be just as important, or even more important, than the type of sales promotion used. Because these consumers are not looking for sales promotions and may also be time-pressed, it may be necessary to catch their attention through some kind of unusual delivery system or creative approach. It also may be the case, however, that some consumers who buy brands out of inertia, if persuaded to try a competitive product, may begin to buy the new brand out of habit in the future. It therefore may prove to be worthwhile to put extra effort into winning over those customers.

Switchers

Switchers or swing users are people who purchase a variety of brands within one category. In general, switchers are much easier to win over with sales promotions than are competitive loyals, as they have purchased a variety of products in the past. However, it may also be the case that since switchers attach less importance to their brand

Exhibit 3.2.   Types of Sales Promotions

Type	Description
Coupon	Certificate allowing consumer to get reduced price at purchase.
Bonus Pack	More product for the regular price.
In-Pack On-Pack, Near-Pack	Gift given to consumers at purchase.
Specialty Container	Container that can be reused or that adds value to the product.
Continuity Program	Reward system for multiple purchases.
Refund	Consumer gets money back after purchase.
Sweepstakes	Consumer has a random chance to win a prize—no purchase required.
Contest	Consumers compete to win a prize—purchase may be required.
Through-the-Mail Premium	Gift given to consumers after the purchase.
Sampling	Product is given to consumers for free.
Price-Off	Product package informs consumer that marked price is lower than regular price.
Trade Deal	Retailer gets discount on price of product or incentive for promoting the product to consumers.

choice, they are not very likely to stick with a particular brand after the promotion is over.

Availability

In certain cases consumers may switch brands because their preferred brand is not readily available. Getting distribution is certainly a difficult issue, and it is one that relies on a variety of factors, such as product mix, previous manufacturer success ratios, manufacturer support for the product, and available retail space. Sales promotion activities do not provide a complete solution to the distribution issue; nevertheless, they may sometimes be helpful in gaining distribution at the retail level.

Trade deals, though reducing the manufacturer margin, may be effective in persuading retailers that it is worth their while to stock a particular brand. Coupons, sampling, sweepstakes, and continuity plans—because they create consumer demand and cause consumers to look for the product (and perhaps complain when it's not available)—may also be helpful in certain circumstances. However, price-offs, refunds, bonus packs, and other promotions that consumers find out about in-store will not usually create consumer demand or increase distribution, since if the brands and promotions are not in the store, consumers have no way of learning about them. And specialty packaging—which may in some cases be odd-sized and difficult to fit on a store shelf or in the warehouse—may actually detract from the chance of getting good distribution.

Value Buyers

Often when consumers switch back and forth among different brands, it is because they are not particularly committed to any of them and simply choose the one that appears to be the best deal at the time from all products in the category or from a set of preselected brands. Although they may prefer certain brands over others, those considerations are outweighed by price some or all of the time.

Because these consumers are interested in value, promotions that lower the price of the brand may be very effective. These may include coupons (provided that the consumer in question clips coupons), rebates, trade deals, price-offs, or bonus packs. Continuity programs may also be effective in some cases, depending on the perceived value of the item being saved for, since they directly address the habit of switching and give consumers a reward for sticking with one brand.

Other promotions that bring some kind of added value to the brand may also be effective, depending on their desirability. Promotions of this type may include sweepstakes, bonus packs, specialty packaging, and premiums. Point-of-purchase (POP) materials may also be of some use, especially for impulse products, in that they call attention to a particular brand and cause consumers to examine it more closely. (Because consumers may still be looking for value, however, it may be most effective to pair POP materials with another type of promotion, such as a price-off or specialty package, for maximum effectiveness.)

Sampling probably will not provide much motivation to these customers, unless they have never tried a particular brand before.

Occasion Usage

One of the reasons that consumers may buy different brands within a category is to fulfill discrete needs. For instance, a woman may consistently buy Diet Coke for herself and Mountain Dew for her husband. If these choices are truly consistent, then these consumers should probably be viewed as brand loyal, and treated as described in the sections on competitive loyals or loyal users.

Variety Seekers

Consumers who switch from one brand to another may have variety as a goal, perhaps in combination with value. Variety is a particularly important issue in several food product categories, where people may get bored with eating the same thing over and over again. It may also be a factor in other industries, such as personal products (fragrances and shampoos, for example) or fashion.

Variety seekers benefit from buying a number of different products. Therefore the goal of sales promotion programs should be to provide the consumer with an incentive to purchase the brand some of the time or at a particular point in time. The good news here is that because these people are interested in having a selection of brands, they may be easily swayed by sales promotion efforts that tip the scales toward a particular brand. By the same token, they are also likely to be easily influenced by promotional efforts for competitive brands, and they probably will not stay with any product after a particular program is over.

Consumers who are interested in variety are likely to exhibit a strong positive reaction to most types of sales promotion programs. Price promotions (either in-store or through coupons) are likely to elicit large amounts of increased sales from those variety seekers who are price sensitive. Promotions that add extra value to the brand and make it appear more fun may also be useful—sweepstakes and contests, bonus packs, specialty packaging, and premiums are all good examples of this tendency. Point-of-purchase materials, because they attract the consumer's attention to the brand, may also be effective. Probably the only types of programs that would be considered generally ineffective at reaching this kind of consumer would be continuity programs (since consumers desiring variety would not want to commit themselves to one product) and sampling (because consumers may have already tried most of the brands on the market).

Price Buyers

Price buyers are people who consistently purchase the lowest-price brand on the market. This may mean that they consistently buy one brand, if it is always the least expensive, or they may switch among brands as their prices change.

Price buyers may be affected by price promotions, but only if the promotions reduce the price of the brand to match that of the competitive brand that would have been purchased instead. This can generally be accomplished through coupons, price-offs, refunds, or trade deals that are passed on to the consumer. Other promotions that add value, such as bonus packs, continuity plans, specialty packaging, premiums, and extra product may occasionally be successful in winning these customers, but they generally are much less effective.

Because these consumers are looking solely at price, they will purchase the brand only during the promotion. After the promotion, they nearly always will return to whatever other brand is the cheapest.

Nonusers

Nonusers are people who don't use any product in the category. As such, they are particularly resistant to most sales promotion activities.

One of the reasons that sales promotions work so poorly at affecting nonusers of a product category is that these types of people generally have negative attitudes about the category as a whole. Before sales promotion can work to influence behavior, it is necessary to change those negative attitudes, perhaps with the use of advertising, personal selling, public relations, or positive word of mouth.

Price Problems

In a few cases, especially with high-cost items, nonusers might want to purchase a product but simply find it too expensive. In those cases it is possible to use price promotions to increase sales, but only if the price discounts are substantial. For instance, Jaguar might attract a number of nonusers of luxury automobiles if it offered a $10,000 rebate on each car purchased. However, since this kind of discounting cuts substantially into profit margins, most companies are willing to do it only in extreme circumstances.

Value

Some people could afford to purchase a particular type of product but don't think that it's worth the price. Sampling may sometimes cause these people to reconsider a product's value, if they haven't tried a particular brand before; they may also, in a few select circumstances, take advantage of a large price discount or a particularly attractive peripheral offer, such as a sweepstakes or specialty package or premium. However, again, since these people have failed to use a type of product in the past, they probably will be unmoved by most promotions for items in that category.

Lack of Need

Some nonusers either may perceive that they really don't need a particular type of product or may actually have no use whatsoever for it. Consumers who see no value in a particular product may occasionally be persuaded otherwise with the use of a sample, but this is relatively rare. And people who actually have no use for a product (for instance, people without lawns do not need lawn mowers) will certainly be uninfluenced by any type of sales promotion.

How to Use the Behavior Analysis Model

In planning a more strategic sales promotion program, marketers will do well to first investigate the overall pattern of consumption in the category and the relative position of each of the customer groups within that category. For instance, in some categories nearly all customers are switchers, while in others many consumers stick with one particular brand. In other categories, particularly those that are in the growth stage, a large percentage of the population may be nonusers but nonetheless have some potential for future consumption.

It is also important to look at each brand individually. For instance, a widely recognized brand may work to capitalize on the goodwill of its brand loyal customers, whereas a relatively unknown brand that's trying to grow may need to focus most of its attention on stealing share from switchers or competitive loyals. In some categories, such as laundry detergent, a percentage of consumers may be loyal to one particular brand, while others switch back and forth between two or more brands. Understanding what is going on in the marketplace is the first step toward using sales promotion to achieve certain goals. This type of information is increasingly available through scanner data provided by such companies as Information Resources Inc. (IRI) and A.C. Nielsen.

The second step is to try to understand why consumers behave the way they do. For instance, consumers who never buy a particular brand because they believe that it is of poor quality should not be expected to purchase it just because the manufacturer drops a high-value coupon for it. In order to change those consumers' behavior, the marketer will first need to change their attitudes, perhaps through product reformulation, advertising, public relations, or a sampling program. On the other hand, consumers who fail to buy a brand because they have forgotten about it, or because they think it's too expensive, or because they have grown used to buying a different brand may be appropriate targets for the right sales promotion programs. This kind of information about the market as a whole must generally be gathered through some sort of qualitative research, such as a focus group, survey, in-depth interview, or observational study.

Exhibit 3.3　Types of Consumers and Appropriate Promotions

Promotions

Consumer Types	Coupons	Special Packs	Sampling	Contests/ Sweepstakes	Continuity	Refunds	Price-Offs	Premiums	Trade Deals
CURRENT LOYALS: Reinforced	Strong	Strong	Limited	Strong	Strong	Strong	Strong	Strong	Strong
Extra Sales	Moderate	Strong	None	Strong (depends)	Strong	Moderate	Strong	Moderate	Strong
Crossover Sales	Moderate	Strong	—	Strong (depends)	Strong	Moderate	—	Strong	—
COMPETITIVE LOYALS: Intense Loyals	None	None	Limited	Limited	None	None	None	Limited	None
Value Seekers	Limited	Limited	Moderate	Limited	Limited	Limited	None	Limited	Limited
Inertia	Limited	Limited	Strong	Strong	Moderate	Limited	None	Moderate	Limited
SWITCHERS: Value	Strong	Strong	Strong	Strong	Strong	Strong	Strong	Strong	Strong
Variety	Strong	Strong	None	Strong	None	Strong	Strong	Strong	Strong
Distribution	Moderate	None	Strong	Limited	Moderate	Limited	None	None	Moderate
PRICE BUYERS: Price	Strong	Limited	Limited	Limited	Limited	Strong	Limited	Limited	Strong
NON-USERS: Price	Limited	None	None	None	None	Moderate	None	None	Limited
Value	Limited	None	Limited	Limited	Limited	Moderate	None	Limited	Limited
Lack of Need	None	None	None	None	None	None	None	None	None

◯ = positive residual value may be created

The third step is to determine what types of promotional activities that competitors have begun or are planning and the effects these activities are likely to have on the marketplace. Knowledge of competitive activities in the areas of product development, advertising, sales promotion, packaging, public relations, trade activities, and geographic targeting can be acquired by observing the marketplace, monitoring trade publications, keeping in touch with retailers, carefully examining scanner data for changes in trends, and simply imagining what actions competitors are likely to take based on their current management, financial constraints, and the situation in the marketplace. Scanner data from past promotions can enable marketers to predict what effects specific competitive activities are likely to have on the marketplace. Armed with this information, marketers will be better prepared to use sales promotion or other tools to effectively counter those activities.

The fourth step in planning a sales promotion program is to determine the program's goals—that is, to determine whether the program is designed to increase profits over the short term or the long term and which types of consumers are to be targeted. Generally, most sales promotion programs are successful either at increasing the long-term potential of the brand or at producing short-term profits, but not both. Thus it is important to determine what the purpose of a particular sales promotion effort is supposed to be. Marketers should also decide what types of consumers (such as loyal users, switchers, competitive loyals, or nonusers of the category) need to be targeted, and which types of sales promotion tactics will work best to accomplish the desired goals.

In short, this book is not designed to provide marketers with "rules" about how to use sales promotions, because every situation is different and therefore will require individual understanding and planning. Instead, it is intended to give some generalized theories on how specific sales promotion tactics work and on when they tend to be most appropriate. Armed with that information and with knowledge of the specific situation confronting a particular brand, marketers will then be able to create programs individually tailored to their particular needs.

Other Issues Involved with the Behavior Analysis Model

A model such as the one described may seem, at least on paper, simple to understand and use. It may even appear that all that marketers need to do is determine the type of customers they want to reach, and then simply conduct the appropriate promotional activities to reach those targets.

However, the model—and the field of sales promotion—is not that simplistic. Therefore it is important to recognize the stumbling blocks that marketers may face when conducting sales promotion activities.

One issue is that consumer behavior in most categories is generally in a state of flux. Individual consumers may move in and out of different categories as their needs or life-styles change. (To take two obvious examples, a man may start clipping coupons when he loses his job, and nonusers of diapers will start buying them when they have children.) In addition, the composition of behaviors in the entire category may change, due to changes in life-styles, the economy, competition, or other factors. Therefore marketers need to carefully monitor the marketplace in order to keep up-to-date on any changes that might be occurring.

Another major problem is that sales promotions aimed at one segment of the marketplace will often be seen and, perhaps, used by everyone in the market. In many cases this does not matter; in other cases, however, excessive redemption of the promotion by the wrong group may nullify any positive immediate profits. Probably the most common example of this is when marketers use high-value coupons or other price promotions to try to lure competitive users to try their brands, in the hope that they will purchase them again in the future. What usually happens is that few competitive users take advantage of the coupons, while many, many current users (most of whom might have purchased the products anyway) redeem them. This kind of issue is slowly being addressed by new forms of consumer targeting and distribution such as direct marketing; nevertheless, it remains a crucial issue.

Finally, although sales promotion is discussed in this book as if it will always be used by itself, it should be realized that sales promotion can often be especially effective when paired with other types of marketing activities, especially those that affect consumer attitudes, such as product changes, advertising, or public relations. For example, a new or reformulated brand that addresses competitive loyals in advertising by describing the product advantages may benefit from using sales promotion, such as coupons, to encourage purchase. Therefore, when developing their sales promotion programs, marketers should consider everything else that is happening with their own brands as well as with competitive products.

The Issue of Payout

Another crucial point in the use of promotional techniques is the widespread belief that the individual promotion, because its effects tend to be short term, must provide increased profits during the life of the promotion.

Because this book is intended to be an overview of the field of sales promotion, the complicated and technical issues of how to estimate payout will not be covered here in an in-depth fashion. Nevertheless, most marketers who conduct sales promotion programs do look at the issue of payout, and so its value and limitations should be understood.

Basically, payout means that promotional programs should result in increased profits *during the time period during, and immediately following the promotion.* The cost of the promotion is compared with the extra profits generated by the incremental value due to the promotional activity.

In order to predict payout, it is first necessary to estimate the profits that would have been made during a period of time if the promotion hadn't been run. The period of time measured usually includes the time during the promotion as well as some length of time following it, for the reason that promotions usually "cannibalize" future sales because consumers tend to stock up on promoted items and therefore do not need to purchase them again for a while. (This effect may even be seen in industries where consumers cannot stock up on the item; for instance, people who have eaten at Burger King several times in one week may tire of the food and not want to eat there again for a while.)

In certain cases, too, especially when promotional periods can be predicted by consumers, the time period *before* the promotion occurs may be examined. This is because if consumers can predict that a promotion may occur, they may wait to buy the product. For instance, some consumers may realize that Coca-Cola goes on special every few weeks in one store or another, and they may therefore buy only a minimal amount of the product until they can get it on deal. Other people may realize that certain department store cosmetics counters have "bonus days" every season, and they may wait for those times to purchase needed items. The length of the time period that must be examined varies from category to category, and it is dependent on ordinary purchase behaviors and on the perishability and bulkiness of the product.

Once the "regular" profits are estimated, they should be compared with the anticipated profits of the same period of time if the promotion is run. Increasingly, this number can be accurately predicted by using mathematical models derived from previous brand activities. Although these types of models can be fairly complicated, they usually take into consideration the type, amount, and length of the promotion, as well as other relevant factors.

Obviously, sales promotions involve trade-offs. In the case of price promotions, increased volume is paired with decreased profit margin. With other promotions, such as sweepstakes, increased volume is countered by the overhead (or fixed costs) of the sales promotion. Therefore each promotion needs to be analyzed beforehand to determine if it really appears to be worthwhile. Promotions should also be evaluated after they are over, to make certain that they did indeed pay out.

The reason that payout is so important in the field of sales promotion is that results of promotions are often assumed to be short term. In contrast with advertising and other activities that affect attitudes and that may therefore influence sales far into the future, the behavior-oriented discipline of sales promotion is often assumed to have no long-term effects. Therefore profits must be gained now or never.

This generalization is much too bold, however. There are several cases when sales promotion *can* affect long-term sales and can change the residual market value and relationship value of the brand. When this is the case, immediate payout may not always be necessary, as the following examples illustrate.

1. Sampling may convince people of a brand's merits, and because of this attitude change these consumers may continue to buy the product over and over again in the future. Therefore sampling is rarely expected to show immediate payout. Instead, it is usually considered one of the expenses of launching a brand, similar to advertising or slotting allowances (the one-time fee that manufacturers pay retailers for adding a product to their distribution).

2. Certain promotions, such as high-value coupons or other price promotions, may cause consumers to try brands that they have never used before. If this occurs and consumers' attitudes are favorably influenced, then that promotion will have created long-term value.

3. Sometimes people may change their behavior because of a promotion, then stick with that brand out of inertia. This means that long-term value has been created, because consumers are continuing to buy the product without additional promotion. (The frequency of this kind of occurrence is uncertain, however; more research needs to be done on this topic.)

4. Sometimes promotion may reinforce current loyals' behavior and keep them from trying other brands in the face of competitive promotion. This theory assumes that consumers who try competitive brands may continue to use those products in the future. If a manufacturer's own promotion can keep its loyal customers from trying those other products, then those people may be more likely to stick with their current brand in the future. (Again, it is not known exactly how often this particular scenario occurs.)

5. Promotion may sometimes persuade a retailer to stock a particular brand or to reconsider discontinuing it. For instance, if many consumers attempt to use a coupon for a brand or if the retailer gets a big trade deal, increased distribution that will continue even after the promotion is over may be gained.

6. Occasionally consumers may get used to buying a larger size or more containers of a brand during a promotional period. If that product is easily consumed, the larger amount may continue to be purchased on a regular basis even after the promotion is over. For instance, consider a woman who usually buys one 12-pack of Pepsi Cola for her family per week. If one week a 24-pack is on sale and if the family easily consumes it by the end of the week, she may decide to purchase a 24-pack every week into the future. (Again, it's uncertain how often this trade-up behavior occurs.)

7. Sometimes a promotion may result in actual improved customer feeling about a brand. For instance, an interesting sweepstakes may result in long-term awareness and goodwill, particularly if the consumer wins some sort of prize. Premiums (say, a Budweiser beach towel) may act as long-term reminders and goodwill builders. Certainly, event and cause marketing results in positive consumer awareness and attitudes, which may translate into long-term sales.

8. Companies that engage in frequent price discounting may find that their long-term brand value may deteriorate due to the promotion. This may be because consumers start to view the discounted price as the "real" price and become unwilling to pay the full regular price in the future. (A case in point is the airline industry, where discounts have taught consumers that they should never pay full price.) Some researchers also theorize that consumers may look at a brand that's always on deal and wonder what's wrong with the product, decreasing the relationship value of the brand.

Because sales promotion activities may have these types of effects on the long-term success of brands, marketers should weigh all of their implications when planning promotional programs. Looking only at short-term profits can cause marketers to miss some of the long-term advantages or liabilities inherent in their programs.

Chapter Four

Coupons

Coupons are by far the most popular and relied-upon form of consumer sales promotion in the United States. More than 270 billion manufacturer-originated coupons were distributed to consumers in 1990, up from only 96 billion in 1980. Consumers saved about $3.5 billion by redeeming 7 billion coupons in 1990.

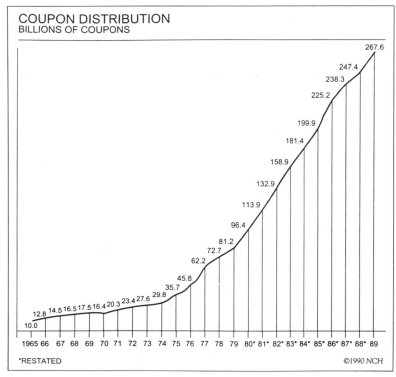

COUPON DISTRIBUTION
BILLIONS OF COUPONS

267.6
247.4
238.3
225.2
199.9
181.4
158.9
132.9
113.9
96.4
81.2
72.7
62.2
45.8
35.7
29.8
27.6
23.4
20.3
16.4
17.5
16.5
14.5
12.8
10.0

1965 66 67 68 69 70 71 72 73 74 75 76 77 78 79 80* 81* 82* 83* 84* 85* 86* 87* 88* 89

*RESTATED   ©1990 NCH

Exhibit 4.1. Billions of Coupons Distributed
Source: NCH Promotional Services.

Coupons have often been thought of as certificates that entitle the consumer to some sort of incentive to buy a product. Although that incentive is usually a reduction in the price of the product at the retail level, coupons can also be used to deliver refunds, combination offers, free samples, or other types of promotions.

Coupons are generally divided into two basic types: (1) trade-originated and (2) manufacturer-originated. Trade-originated coupons are redeemable only at a particular store or group of stores, and they are designed to get consumers to shop at that retail outlet and hopefully to purchase impulse items when inside.

Manufacturer-originated coupons, on the other hand, are distributed by the maker or marketer of the product. They usually may be redeemed at any retailer that carries the product; the retailer then receives reimbursement for the face value of the coupon plus a handling fee.

Although most of this chapter will concentrate on manufacturer-originated coupons, much of this discussion—including distribution channels and consumer buying behavior—can also be applied to those that are trade-originated. Trade coupons will be discussed further in Chapter 12.

Consumer Usage

Perhaps the best answer to the question "What type of person uses coupons?" would simply be "Everybody." About 77 percent of Americans use coupons at least occasionally (compared to 75 percent in 1984 and only 58 percent in 1971), and usage tends to be fairly independent of age, income, education, life-style, race, and gender, according to Manufacturers Coupon Control Center. Although some experts believe that coupon usage is affected by the "smart shopper syndrome" (that is, the amount of personal satisfaction that an individual, regardless of income, gets from saving money), it is generally difficult to predict whether particular consumers will use coupons simply by looking at their demographic characteristics.

Although most consumers use coupons occasionally, a much smaller percentage uses them on a regular basis. In general, women tend to use coupons more frequently than do men, but that is probably because women do routine shopping more often than men; men and women are almost equally likely to be heavy coupon users. People in certain areas of the country are more likely to clip coupons, and coupon usage increases somewhat with age. Heavy users of coupons are more likely to have children, to have high grocery bills, and to live in the suburbs; perhaps surprisingly, they are also more likely to have high incomes.

Evidence suggests that consumers are more likely to use coupons during a recession or when they personally are worried about their

Exhibit 4.2. Coupon Use by Demographics

	% Who use coupons	% Heavy users	Average number of coupons used per week
All respondents	77%	29%	8
By sex			
Female	82%	29%	8
Male	56%	25%	6
By ethnicity			
White/ Non-Hispanic	78%	28%	8
Black/ Non-Hispanic	71%	31%	8
Hispanic	70%	30%	7
By age			
18-24	66%	38%	10
25-30	74%	26%	7
31-35	82%	38%	9
36-45	74%	40%	9
46-60	80%	23%	7
61 +	80%	14%	5

Source: Courtesy of Manufacturers Coupon Control Center, Clinton, Iowa.

Exhibit 4.3. Coupon Use by Geography

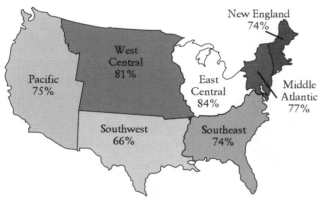

	% Heavy users	Average number of coupons used per week
Pacific	21%	6
West Central	16%	6
Southwest	32%	7
East Central	29%	8
Southeast	28%	8
New England	28%	8
Middle Atlantic	40%	9

Source: Courtesy of Manufacturers Coupon Control Center, Clinton, Iowa.

Exhibit 4.4.   Typical Coupon User Profile

Sex:	Female
Average weekly grocery expenditures:	$74
Average weekly coupon savings:	$6
Median age:	45
Education:	More than likely high school graduate with some college education.
Employment:	More than likely employed full time, but could also be a homemaker, or retired.
Marital status:	More than likely married.
Ethnic origin:	More than likely White/non-Hispanic
Median household income:	$29,000
Number of people in household:	3
Number of employed people in household:	1.5

Source: Courtesy of Manufacturers Coupon Control Center, Clinton, Iowa.

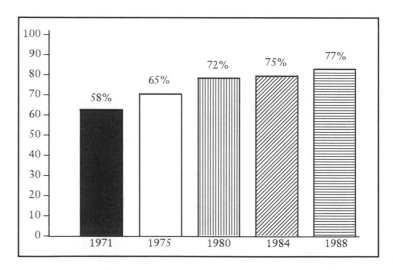

Exhibit 4.5.   Percentage of Households Using Coupons
Source: Courtesy of Manufacturers Coupon Control Center, Clinton, Iowa.

future. This tendency may again tie in with the so-called "smart shopper syndrome": People who are anxious about their financial future may gain some sense of control when they save money, no matter how small the amount or how large their current incomes.

More than 3,000 manufacturers in the United States offer coupons to consumers, a figure that is up 50 percent from 1980. Although consumer redemption of coupons seems to have plateaued at around 7 billion in the late 1980s (see Exhibit 4-7), manufacturers continue to offer an increasing number of coupons each year. As a result, the percentage of coupons redeemed has dropped slightly in the last few years.

Coupons have become popular promotional tools with manufacturers for a variety of reasons:

- Coupons provide a means of distributing a price cut to consumers, who have become increasingly price sensitive and less brand loyal.

- Unlike regular price cuts, coupons may make consumers feel that they are getting a good deal on a particular product, thereby causing them to increase consumption.

- Also unlike regular price cuts, coupons provide temporary price reductions; the brand returns to the regular price after the expiration date.

- Coupons may encourage new consumers to try a product, increasing the value of the brand over the long run.

- Coupons ensure that price cuts are passed on to the consumer. (Often, retailers who receive a decrease in their wholesale price of a product may absorb it as extra margin rather than reducing the retail price on the shelf and passing the savings on to the consumer.)

- Coupons may be effective in differentiating between price-sensitive and price-insensitive consumers. Those who are price

Increase in Manufacturers' Use of Coupons

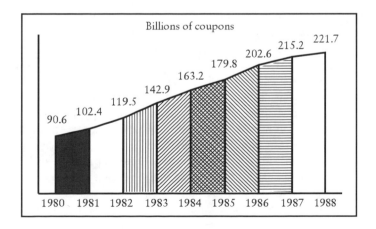

Exhibit 4.6. Coupons Distributed
Source: Courtesy of Manufacturers Coupon Control Center, Clinton, Iowa.

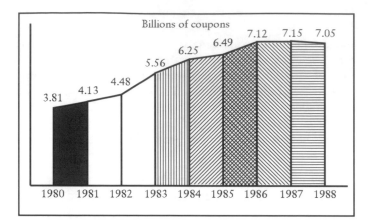

Exhibit 4.7.   Coupons Redeemed
Source: Courtesy of Manufacturers Coupon Control Center, Clinton, Iowa.

sensitive are assumed to be more likely to clip coupons, whereas those who don't care very much about saving the money are more likely to pay full price.

- Coupon distribution may be easily targeted to particular areas of the country or particular types of consumers, helping companies to accomplish specific targeted marketing goals.

- Coupons may create demand for the product among consumers, making it more likely that the retailer will begin or continue to carry the couponed product.

The issue of bypassing the retailer with the use of coupons is an especially important one to manufacturers of groceries and of health-care and beauty-care products, who are by far the most frequent users of coupons. These kinds of manufacturers have in recent years held decreasing power in comparison to their retailers, who may legally charge consumers whatever they want no matter what price decreases or trade promotions they receive from manufacturers. Coupons have therefore become a good way for manufacturers to influence what consumers pay for their products.

Coupon distribution has been much more prevalent in some categories than in others, and many consumers expect to use a coupon each time they purchase a product in these categories. These categories include a variety of low-involvement, parity brands (such as laundry products, household cleaners, ready-to-eat cereals, and coffee) that are subject to much consumer brand switching. It seems that manufacturers in these categories have often substituted price promotions for brand differentiation.

Although coupons are most often used for price discounts on inexpensive items, they have occasionally been used to promote high-

Exhibit 4.8. Percentage of coupon users who always expect to have a coupon in the following categories

Laundry products	50%
Household cleaners	45%
Ready-to-eat cereals	45%
Coffee	42%
Personal care items	39%
Paper products	34%
Drug products	33%
Frozen foods and entrees	28%
Carbonated beverages	27%
Dairy products	22%
Pet products	22%

Source: Courtesy of Manufacturers Coupon Control Center, Clinton, Iowa.

■■■■■■■■■■■■■■■■■ CLIP AND SAVE ■■■■■■■■■■■■■■■■

SOFTWARE PEOPLE
Clip This Coupon and Redeem It For
$1000
Upon presentation 30 days after starting employment with...AGS

As you can see, we really appreciate professional people! Right now, we're seeking several systems programmers to work on a challenging software development effort for a new computer communications system. We are looking for people with superior design/programming skills and two to twelve years of experience. Experience with operating systems development, real-time systems, specialized telecommunications processors, simulator/emulator development, micro/mini computers, higher level languages and ASSEMBLY languages, ETC. would all be very advantageous.

We will provide you with an outstanding compensation and benefits package. You will work with the best software specialists and hardware engineers in the business. The work is challenging and the opportunities unlimited.

We are a major systems development company with a professional staff of over 400 information systems specialists. In order to sustain our continuing growth, we must add several systems programmers to our staff immediately.

For consideration, please send your resume in complete confidence to: Liz Maynor, Director of Professional Staffing, AGS Computers, Inc., 1301 West 22nd Street, Oakbrook, Illinois 60521.

And Save This Coupon!
AGS Computers, Inc.

Equal Opportunity Employer M/F

■■■■■■■■■■■■■■■■■ CLIP AND SAVE ■■■■■■■■■■■■■■■■

CLIP AND SAVE

Exhibit 4.9. A $1,000 Coupon
Source: Courtesy of AGS Computers, Inc.

value products. For example, Continental Airlines once ran a coupon in a variety of newspapers offering a round-trip ticket anywhere in the United States for $198, good only with the use of the coupon. High-value coupons may have serious problems with misredemption, however, and so coupons for high-priced items are often used to call attention to a special promotion offered through the manufacturer (which may be valid only when the coupon is presented) rather than give a certain amount off a set purchase price through a retailer.

Coupon Delivery

Coupons may be delivered to the consumer through a variety of channels. Some of these deliver coupons to a broad mass audience; others are targeted at specific consumers in order to achieve particular objectives.

Free-Standing Insert (FSI)

By far the most prevalent form of coupon delivery is through the free-standing insert (FSI). About 80 percent of coupons in the United States are distributed through FSIs, which have grown enormously in popularity during the past decade.

FSIs generally consist of $8^{1}/_{2} \times 11$-inch "booklets" of four-color advertisements with coupons that are distributed in Sunday newspapers. Most FSIs are developed as cooperative ventures, with many noncompetitive marketers contributing materials and sharing the

Exhibit 4.10.   Average Coupon Redemption Rates—by Delivery Method

	Grocery Products	Health & Beauty Care
Free-Standing Inserts (FSIs)	2.8%	1.4%
Direct Mail	3.7%	2.4%
ROP Newspaper	1.6%	.3%
Magazine—Pop Up/Insert	1.7%	1.4%
Magazine—Printed on Page	1.2%	.4%
On-Pack (Same Product)	9.6%	8.1%
In-Pack (Same Product)	13.5%	8.0%
On-Pack (Cross-Ruff)	3.5%	5.6%
In-Pack (Cross-Ruff)	3.5%	2.0%
Instant On-Pack	29.1%	43.5%
Handouts	3.2%	1.8%
Electronic	11%	8.5%

Source: NCH Promotional Services.

Exhibit 4.11. Coupon and Recipe as Part of an FSI Advertisement
Source: Courtesy of Lawry's Foods, Inc.; Lea & Perrins.

costs on a proportionate basis. FSIs are often coordinated by an outside firm, which charges marketers for printing and distribution to newspapers. Individual newspapers usually charge a flat fee per thousand to distribute the FSIs to consumers.

FSIs have a number of advantages. They provide a broad distribution at a relatively low price, $7 to $8 per thousand in 1990. Unlike advertisements printed inside the newspaper, FSIs may be

Exhibit 4.12.   FSI Advertisement with Attractive Graphics
Source: Courtesy of American Home Food Products, Inc.

targeted to specific sections of a metropolitan area; they also appear
in color (generating consumer attention and discouraging forgers)
and have room for a selling message and attractive graphics. In
addition, because they consistently appear in the same place in the
paper, they are easy for consumers to find.

FSIs also have disadvantages, but most manufacturers have
evidently decided that the advantages far outweigh them. FSIs may
not make it to the intended target, due either to carelessness on

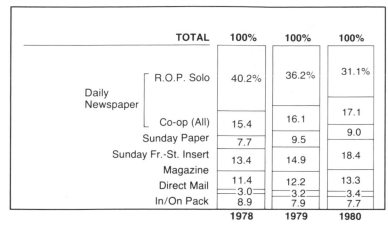

	TOTAL	100%	100%	100%
R.O.P. Solo		40.2%	36.2%	31.1%
Daily Newspaper				
				17.1
Co-op (All)		15.4	16.1	
Sunday Paper		7.7	9.5	9.0
Sunday Fr.-St. Insert		13.4	14.9	18.4
Magazine				
Direct Mail		11.4	12.2	13.3
		3.0	3.2	3.4
In/On Pack		8.9	7.9	7.7
		1978	1979	1980

Exhibit 4.13.   Coupon Distribution by Media
Source: Courtesy of NCH Promotional Services.

the part of the newspaper's circulation department or to theft. Also, because some newspapers may limit the number of insertions they will accept each week, it may sometimes be difficult to get FSIs placed. Finally, since insertions must be printed in advance and shipped to the newspapers, a long lead time is required.

Newspaper Run-of-Press (ROP)

About 6 percent of coupons are distributed run-of-press (ROP), meaning that they are printed inside the newspaper rather than inserted into it. The number of coupons distributed ROP has declined sharply during the past decade as the number of FSIs as increased.

ROP coupons do have some advantages over free-standing inserts. They may be distributed on days other than Sunday, such as on a "best food day," and, since newspapers will generally accept advertising up to a day or two before distribution, lead times are shorter. Also, newspapers are responsible for printing, and distribution of the ROP is more of a guarantee of distribution than with an FSI (which may get lost before it reaches the consumer). However, ROP ads do not usually allow the geographic targeting of FSIs, and they usually cannot be printed in four-color (meaning that they may be easily overlooked by consumers or counterfeited). ROP advertising also tends to be expensive (for example, running an FSI-sized ad inside the paper usually will cost much more than the $7 to $8 per thousand that FSIs cost). In addition, ROP coupons may be easily missed by consumers who don't read the entire paper, or who don't look closely at all the ads.

Exhibit 4.14.   Carol Wright Co-op Service Coupons
Source: Courtesy of Donnelley Marketing.

Direct Mail

About 4 percent of coupons are delivered to consumers through direct delivery, either through the U.S. Postal Service or through an alternative delivery service. Direct-mail coupons may be mailed individually (usually with other selling materials about the product and possibly with a product sample). They may also be delivered as part of a group of coupons; a well-known example of this kind of delivery is the Carol Wright co-op mailing developed by Donnelley Marketing, which includes coupons from a variety of manufacturers.

Delivery of coupons by mail has a number of advantages. Perhaps the most important of these is selectivity: Coupons may be targeted at specific neighborhoods or zip codes, or at people who appear to meet some sort of demographic specification. In addition, marketers who possess lists of their own or of competitors' customers can send coupons directly to these people to fulfill specific marketing objectives.

Perhaps because they are so targeted and because they are more infrequently received by consumers than are FSIs, direct-mail coupons tend to have relatively high redemption rates. Direct mail can also allow coupons to gain broader distribution than FSIs, which are not seen by households that don't receive newspapers. This broad coverage may be important to some manufacturers, particularly during the introduction of new mass-marketed products.

The major disadvantage of using direct-mail couponing is its extremely high delivery cost, which can start at $15 to $20 per

Exhibit 4.15.   National Opinion Survey

thousand but which may be much higher depending on the specificity desired. This high cost includes purchasing mailing lists, printing the materials and envelopes, handling, and postage.

An innovative form of direct-mail coupon distribution was pioneered by a company called Computerized Marketing Technology (CMT). CMT and similar companies distribute detailed questionnaires to consumers, collecting information about the types of products and particular brands that they use, as well as demographic and life-style information. Marketers may then use this information to send coupons or other sales promotion materials directly to precisely targeted groups of these consumers—selecting, for instance, buyers of their competitors' products or such hard-to-reach segments as people with allergies. Coupons distributed through this channel are generally coded, so that marketers can track response rates among various groups.

Although this method can be very effective at targeting specific groups, and although it can be helpful to some companies for re-

Exhibit 4.16.   FSI Coupon
Source: Courtesy of Kellogg Company.

search purposes, it tends to be very expensive—at least $25 per thousand. Another disadvantage of this type of distribution is that a relatively small percentage of households are willing to supply personal information to this type of program, meaning that it is inappropriate for most mass-marketed new products that need to obtain broad-based trial among a large percentage of the population in order to be successful.

Although some manufacturers have made some tentative steps toward using more direct-mail coupons during the past few years, the high cost has prevented it from becoming a very important force. Although direct mail has the potential of targeting consumers on an individual level, few marketers have thus far found it financially rewarding to take advantage of that opportunity.

Magazines

Magazines have decreased in popularity as a coupon delivery medium during the last decade. Currently, only about 3 percent of coupons are delivered through magazines.

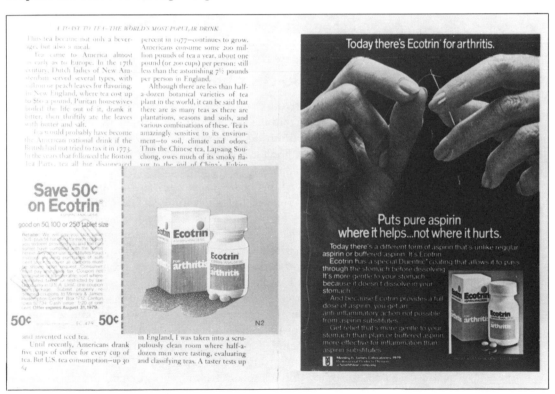

Exhibit 4.17.   Pop-Up Coupon
Source: Courtesy of Menley & James Laboratories.

Magazine coupons may be of two types: on-page and "pop-up." On-page coupons are printed on the pages of the magazine; to use them, consumers must tear or cut out part of the page. Pop-up coupons are generally bound into the magazine next to an advertisement for the product, so that they pop up when the magazine is opened to that page. Pop-up coupons are more easily noticed and removed from the magazine, and generally they have redemption rates that are higher than in-page coupons. (This effectiveness is balanced by higher delivery costs, however.)

Delivery of coupons through magazines, though declining in popularity, has several advantages. Reproduction quality is high. Some magazines may also deliver a targeted audience appropriate to the particular product being promoted—for instance, disposable diapers may be couponed in *Parents* magazine.

Magazines' biggest problems are that individual publications do not have very wide reach and that couponing in multiple magazines will usually result in many consumers receiving more than one coupon. In addition, although some publications offer regional editions, magazines in general require coupons to be dropped on a nationwide basis, which can be inappropriate for some marketing plans. The more targeted magazines can also be much more expensive than FSIs for a similar-sized ad and coupon.

Merchandise-Distributed Coupons

Coupons delivered to consumers in-pack or on-pack make up about 4 percent of all coupons delivered in the United States, a percentage that has declined during recent years.

In-pack coupons are included inside a package, often with a "flag" on the outside of the package calling attention to their presence. Special care must be taken with in-pack coupons, particularly if they are to be included in food products. There are quite stringent Food and Drug Administration restrictions on how and in what form the coupon may be placed in the box, and there may be certain paper and printing requirements as well. (In addition, in-pack coupons are simply inappropriate for certain kinds of products, such as soft drinks or liquid bleach.)

An alternative to the in-pack coupon is the on-pack coupon. On-pack coupons are attached to the package in some way or are printed as part of the package itself.

Coupons included in-pack or on-pack may apply to future purchases of the same product, future purchases of a different product, or (in some on-pack promotions) the current purchase of the product.

Coupons for future purchases of the same product are generally designed to increase brand loyalty, particularly in a category where switching often occurs. For instance, Green Giant may include a coupon in its frozen spinach that can be used toward any Green Giant frozen vegetable, thereby increasing the likelihood that consumers will buy the product rather than a competitive brand in the future.

Coupons for other products—or "cross-ruffs"—are often used to create interest in less popular items made by the same manufacturer. For instance, Kraft might create awareness of a new packaged rice side dish by placing a coupon for it in its popular Kraft American cheese singles. Cross-ruffs are also used when there is a connection between the product being purchased and the one being promoted; for instance, purchasers of nondairy creamer, who are assumed to be coffee drinkers, may be supplied with a coupon for a particular brand of coffee. In categories where variety is a component of purchase behavior, coupons for other brands in the same category may be used; for instance, Kellogg's may place coupons for a new cereal in boxes of Frosted Flakes. Coupons can be cross-ruffed in products made by other manufacturers, but in practice they are usually distributed within products made by the same manufacturer.

"Instant" coupons are attached to the outside of the package, and can be removed by the consumer to be used for an immediate discount on the price of the item currently being purchased. These coupons have an advantage over trade deals that also have the potential of offering instant savings, in that manufacturers can be sure that the discount is passed on to the consumer. However, not all consumers notice instant coupons or bother to use them; although the redemption rate of this kind of coupon (29 percent) is the highest of all distribution types, it is still used by consumers less than a third of the time.

A major advantage of using in-pack and on-pack coupons is that they have practically no delivery cost, since a product that is already being distributed carries them. The "flag" on the front panel of the product can also provide a point of differentiation at the time of purchase, since some consumers may be more likely to buy a product if they can get a coupon. Since the manufacturer controls the distribution of the product, it is possible to restrict where the coupons are dropped. In addition, redemption rates of in-pack and on-pack coupons tend to be high.

On the other hand, in-pack and on-pack coupons for future purchases of the same product attract no new users; they instead reward existing customers who (depending on the circumstances) may or may not buy the product again even without a coupon. In some cases, special equipment or materials may be required to print the coupons on the package, thereby increasing the cost. In-pack coupons may be overlooked by some consumers, and on-pack coupons may sometimes be difficult for them to remove.

Specialty-Distributed Coupons

Although few coupons are currently distributed through specialty means, this type of distribution can be very appropriate in certain situations.

One of the most innovative forms of distributing coupons is electronically at the cash register. With the advent of point-of-purchase electronic scanners at the cash registers, these kinds of machines can automatically distribute coupons to consumers selected by their current purchasing behaviors. For instance, a consumer who buys a can of Folger's coffee might receive a coupon for $1 off a can of Maxwell House coffee; the large discount is intended to be enough to prompt a substitution in the future. In other cases, the fact that a particular product was purchased may suggest that other products may be needed. For instance, a consumer buying baby formula may receive a coupon for Huggies diapers or for a free photo sitting at a nearby Sears store. Electronic coupons generally have very high response rates, due to their precise targeting and their high value.

Some supermarkets and discount stores now offer in-store kiosks where consumers can pick up coupons for products sold in the store. The advantage here is that consumers may obtain coupons at the time of purchase; however, many customers are rushed when inside the store and do not want to take the time to search for appropriate coupons. In addition, because consumers can take as many coupons as they want, it has generally been necessary to restrict their value to a fairly low amount in order to reduce fraud.

Coupons have long been handed out on the street or in other public places, such as in airplanes or movie theaters. However, this type of distribution tends to be expensive and sometimes is annoying to consumers. It is often used in conjunction with sampling programs.

Issues in Couponing

Value

Most consumers appear to have a threshold of value under which they will not use coupons. In a survey conducted by NCH Promotional Services, consumers said they required an average minimum

Exhibit 4.18.   Value Needed to Buy a New Brand

If offered 35 cent coupons—one for his current brand and one for a new brand—which would consumer choose?*	
Usual brand	75%
New brand	16%
What would be the minimum coupon value necessary to induce purchase of new brand instead?	
Would not buy at all	9%
< or = 39 cents	4%
40-49 cents	10%
50 cents	41%
51-99 cents	13%
$1.00	10%

Average minimum value necessary = 58 cents
*Base = Coupon users
Source: Courtesy of Manufacturers Coupon Control Center, Clinton, Iowa.

value of 23 cents before they would use a coupon. For brands they had not tried before, they said they required an average value of 44 cents. However, most studies show that increasing the value of the coupon beyond the threshold does not increase the likelihood that consumers will use a coupon by very much. Therefore marketers should probably try to identify the consumers they want to influence, and to set coupon values near those consumers' thresholds for their products.

Consumers seem to have different expectations for the value of coupons for different categories of products. This appears to be fairly unrelated to the retail price of the products, and it is instead probably determined by the "typical" discounts offered in each category. Discounts on ready-to-eat cereals tend to be larger than those on household cleaners, for example.

The average value of manufacturer-distributed coupons has gone up sharply during the past several years. In 1989, the average value of coupons for grocery products was 49.2 cents; for health and beauty care products, the average value was 51.5 cents.

A primary reason that most coupons today are of relatively high value is that many manufacturers use them as tools to introduce users of competitive products to the brand. Although the number of consumers who switch only if a coupon is of high value may be few, those people are much less likely to be regular users of the product, and getting them to become triers may result in long-term value. Using high-value coupons may be a conscious decision of marketers

Exhibit 4.19.   Face Value Expectations by Category

Laundry products	59 cents
Pet products	59 cents
Drug products	55 cents
Coffee	53 cents
Carbonated beverages	42 cents
Household cleaners	41 cents
Ready-to-eat cereals	40 cents
Personal care items	39 cents
Frozen food and entrees	39 cents
Dairy products	30 cents
Paper products	30 cents

Source: Courtesy of Manufacturers Coupon Control Center, Clinton, Iowa.

to sacrifice profits on a single coupon drop in exchange for increased trial and brand loyalty.

The Message

While coupons may be of any size or shape, advertisers usually try to make them the shape of a dollar bill. This makes them easier for the consumer, the retailer, and the clearing house to handle. While there are no specific physical requirements for coupons, the cardinal rule is: *If it is a coupon, make it look like a coupon.*

An important part of the coupon is what is called the "boilerplate," or details of the offer. This is simply the copy that explains the coupon to both the consumer and the retailer. This information may appear on the front or (sometimes) the back of the coupon.

Coupons should make the offer boldly and clearly, expressly stating the limitations. It is also worth noting that placing too many restrictions on usage (such as requiring that only certain products in a line or certain sizes are eligible) may not produce the anticipated results, because the retailer (who has no incentive to make sure that the coupon is redeemed properly) may allow consumers to use a coupon even if the exact product specified isn't purchased or even stocked in the store. Therefore keeping the offer simple may help to ensure that the anticipated success will be achieved.

One new type of coupon attempts to turn coupon usage into a "game" by covering the printed value of the discount with a material to be rubbed off or otherwise removed, either at home or in the retail store. Although this type of coupon is new and hasn't been tested much, it appears that many consumers may be willing to uncover the amount to determine how much they have "won." It is less likely

Exhibit 4.20.   A Coupon "Game" Circular
Source: Courtesy of Sears, Roebuck and Co.

that consumers will visit a store to determine the value of their coupons, and some customers may even be annoyed by this type of promotion.

Coupon Redemption

One of the great uncertainties of sales promotion is the rate at which product coupons will be redeemed. Although averages for different kinds of delivery methods have been determined, redemption rates can also depend on specific factors affecting the category, brand, and consumer.

For instance, products that are used by only a small percentage of the population (such as denture cream) will obviously have a smaller redemption rate than products that are used by almost everyone (such as laundry detergent), all else being equal. Placing restrictions on product size can decrease redemption, as may offering a low face value or small percentage of the total purchase price. (For instance, offering a $5 discount on a new car is not likely to excite many consumers.) The amount of brand loyalty in the category and the degree (and appropriateness) of the selection of the delivery process can also be important factors, as can the area of the country in which the coupon is delivered. Retail distribution of the product is also a big factor, since consumers may throw away coupons for brands they can't find in the store. The share of the market of a particular product, the competitive activity in the category, and the degree of product familiarity also may have some effect on redemption rates, although these factors appear to be less important.

Misredemption

Misredemption of coupons can be a serious problem, particularly for companies that distribute high-value coupons. Coupon misredemption may sometimes occur because of carelessness on the part of the retailer; in other cases it may be much more deliberate and methodical.

Since retailers are being reimbursed for the full amount of the coupon, they often are not as careful about redeeming them as they might be if the money were coming out of their own pockets. For example, a harried grocery store clerk who is presented with 20 coupons and $150 worth of groceries is unlikely to check to make certain that all the coupons are for items actually being purchased, since doing so would slow down the line and annoy customers. In addition, retailers and consumers may be lax about checking that the correct size or variety of an item is purchased or that the coupon has not expired.

A second way that coupons may be misredeemed is through organized "gang punching." Gang punchers steal or otherwise obtain great quantities of FSIs and punch out the coupons. Those coupons are then redeemed through unscrupulous retailers or through phony store addresses. (In a few cases, too, dishonest retailers may pay consumers who don't use the coupon a percentage of its face value, then redeem it for the full amount from the manufacturer.)

Although laxness on the part of retailers can be a major problem, most manufacturers have devoted a relatively small amount of resources to confronting this issue. Because these misredemptions tend to be scattered among many retailers, they are hard to spot; in addition, making too big a deal of this issue may jeopardize marketers' relationships with legitimate and important retailers. One way that the problem is being addressed is by retailers who scan coupons at the checkout counter; if the coupon does not match a purchase, then it is not accepted. Marketers who are concerned about misredemptions by their legitimate retailers should include bar codes on their coupons, and they might consider offering some kind of incentive to retailers who scan coupons.

Manufacturers have clamped down much harder on organized coupon misredemptions. Marketers are on the lookout for coupons that appear to be too neatly and uniformly cut out; for stores that have a higher-than-expected volume of coupon redemptions; and for new retailers at unverified addresses. Nevertheless, organized misredemptions remain a major problem for coupon issuers.

The following points may be helpful for marketers who hope to minimize misredemptions:

- Make coupons difficult to duplicate or counterfeit, perhaps by the use of four-color printing or a special kind of paper.
- Treat coupons as money.
- Make certain that expiration dates are easy to find and read.
- Avoid using excessive values in coupons; keep them within reason.
- Avoid using values that exceed the cost of the media in which the coupons are distributed or that exceed the value of the product.
- Keep the offer clear and uncomplicated, making it easy for consumers and retailers to understand.
- Set a redemption policy and stick to it; don't hesitate to refuse payment for redemptions that are clearly fraudulent.
- Match coupon redemptions with store sales to spot stores with unusually high redemption rates.

Multiple-Purchase Coupons

Multiple-purchase coupons require consumers to buy more than one product in order to get a discount. As might be expected, their redemption rates are typically much lower than those of single-

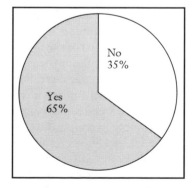

Exhibit 4.21.   Consumers Who Have Used Multiple-Purchase Coupons*
*Base = Coupon users
Source: Courtesy of Manufacturers Coupon Control Center, Clinton, Iowa.

purchase coupons; nevertheless, they can be useful in certain situations (such as to encourage consumers of one popular product to try another one), particularly if a large value is offered.

About 65 percent of coupon users report having used a multiple-purchase coupon; as expected, heavy coupon users are more likely to have done so. These types of coupons tend to be most successful when they are used to promote products in frequently purchased, nonperishable categories, such as paper and laundry products, personal-care items, carbonated beverages, and household cleaners.

Costs

There are two types of costs connected with coupons: those involved with distribution and those involved with redemption. Distribution costs are incurred in getting the coupons to the consumer, such as printing and distribution costs (for instance, placing the print ad or FSI, or postage for direct mail). Redemption costs are associated with the payment and allocation of the discount to the consumer, the retailer, and any middlemen.

Determining distribution costs is straightforward and can easily be done in advance of the execution of the program. Most companies or publications offering coupon distribution quote on a cost per thousand basis, making media relatively easy to compare. Marketers must only be certain that everything (such as printing costs, list rental, or postage) is included.

Redemption costs are more tricky, since they require marketers to estimate how many people will actually redeem the coupon. Because that cannot always be predicted accurately (especially for new products or for those in categories where competitive activities have changed), budgeting for this portion of couponing costs can sometimes be uncertain. Nevertheless, an anticipated redemption rate range can usually be predicted with considerable accuracy.

Redemption costs usually consist of the face value of the coupon plus the various costs of the redemption process. Normally, in addition to the discount given to consumers, retailers are allowed a set price per coupon redeemed to cover handling costs. Handling costs paid to retailers in 1991 were 8 cents per coupon.

Because of the large volume of coupons redeemed by the 30,000 or so mass retailers in the United States, manufacturers do not deal individually with each retailer. Instead, manufacturers and retailers both use clearinghouses, which act in a similar fashion to banks in making payments and clearing documents. Retailers generally forward their coupons to a retailer clearinghouse, which pays them the face value of the coupon and the handling charge. The retail clearinghouse then forwards the coupons to the clearinghouse hired by the manufacturer. The manufacturer clearinghouse checks the coupons for their validity and reimburses the retail clearinghouse. The manufacturer pays fees of between $6.25 to $13 per thousand to the retail clearinghouse and $45 to $50 per thousand to the manufacturer clearinghouse.

As an example, a coupon for 50 cents may generate 100,000 redemptions, half of which were incremental volume (meaning that the product wouldn't have been sold without the coupon). Total redemption costs would be $63,200 (50 cents face value + 8 cents retailer handling fee times 100,000 redemptions plus $700 for retail clearinghouse fees plus $4,500 for manufacturer clearinghouse fees). A typical distribution cost for this type of response might be $35,000, bringing the total cost of the promotion to $98,200.

Typically, these distribution and redemption costs are compared with the incremental profits generated by the increased volume from the coupon. In this example, assume that the manufacturer's profit on each item sold is 75 cents. This amount is then multiplied by the incremental volume generated by the coupon (in this instance, 75 cents × 50,000 = $37,500). This total can be compared to the cost of the promotion to judge whether it provided immediate additional profits.

However, this type of profit analysis leaves out the important issue of residual value of coupon promotions. Often, coupon programs are designed to generate consumer trial at an immediate loss in profits, in the hope that some of the triers will purchase the product at full price in the future. Therefore, even though some coupon promotions may appear at first to be unprofitable, they may actually be very valuable to the brand over the long run.

Expiration Dates

The trend in couponing is definitely moving toward more limited redemption periods. For example, in 1985 more than 23 percent of all coupons were distributed with no expiration date, compared to just under 9 percent in 1988. In contrast, 23 percent of all coupons distributed in 1985 had short expiration dates (less than three months), versus more than 43 percent in 1988. (Source: Manufacturers Coupon Control Center.) The average redemption period dropped to 5 months in 1990 from 6.8 months in 1987, according to NCH Promotional Services.

There are several reasons for the trend toward shorter redemption periods. For one thing, limiting the time span during which a coupon can be redeemed may help marketing managers plan better, and it may allow them to better judge the results of their promotional activities. In addition, shorter redemption periods help to limit a company's financial liabilities, which may be important for accounting reasons.

Most important, however, is that movement to shorter redemption periods can affect the profile of the consumer using the coupon. Often, consumers who stockpile coupons and use them long after they have been distributed are people who either use the product regularly already, or are very promotion sensitive and buy *only* on deal. Limiting the amount of time during which coupons can be redeemed appears to make it more likely that people who redeem the coupons will be those who do not already buy the product, and who may continue to purchase it in the future even without the coupon.

The trend toward shorter redemption periods should not be taken as a hard-and-fast rule, however, since there are some situations when a longer redemption period may make sense. For instance, in-pack and on-pack coupons may not be found or used by consumers for a long time; therefore expiration dates should usually be at least a year or two after the product is distributed. Coupons for infrequently purchased products may also sometimes have longer redemption periods, in order to give the consumer more time to replenish the product.

The Strategic Uses of Coupons

Used properly, coupons can be an effective way to achieve a variety of strategic objectives with many different kinds of consumers.

Loyal Users

Coupons can be very effective at reinforcing sales from loyal users. Coupons targeted at loyal users may be placed in-pack or on-pack; consumers who are coupon sensitive are also likely to use coupons distributed through other channels. Whether these consumers would have purchased the brand anyway, and whether loyals will be more likely to purchase the brand in the future without a coupon, however, is less clear-cut.

Coupons may, in some cases, encourage consumers to purchase a larger size of the product than they might ordinarily. For instance, a consumer who might ordinarily buy a small package of Oreo cookies might be persuaded to buy a bigger package if a coupon is valid only on the larger size. (Coupons for large product sizes may result in much lower overall redemption rates, however.)

Current customers may be persuaded to purchase additional products with the use of cross-ruff in-pack or on-pack coupons. This

Exhibit 4.22. Brand Loyals and Coupons

Will a coupon induce a brand loyal coupon user to try a different brand?	
Definitely	6%
Probably	33%
Maybe	37%
Probably not	16%
Definitely not	6%

Source: Courtesy of Manufacturers Coupon Control Center, Clinton, Iowa.

generally works best when the two products are somehow related to one another, or when purchase of one makes it more likely that another may be needed. For instance, a diaper package may include a coupon for baby wipes.

Coupons targeted directly at loyal users (for instance, through on-packs or electronically at the cash register) may be of low value or for multiple purchases, since these people are unlikely to need very much incentive to be persuaded to buy the brands again.

Competitive Loyals

Consumers who are intensely loyal to a particular product are unlikely to be influenced by a coupon for another brand, but people who are only moderately brand loyal may be influenced by coupons. In a survey conducted by Manufacturers Coupon Control Center, more than 75 percent of consumers who were loyal to a particular product stated that they might be willing to purchase another brand if they received a coupon for it. However, these people are likely to switch only if the coupon is of high value.

Although these consumers may well go back to their former brand the next time they make a purchase after using a coupon for a competitive product, it is possible that they will like the product and continue to use it. In addition, the simple act of buying another product may break their habitual pattern and make them more likely to try other brands in the future.

Switchers

Consumers who buy a variety of brands tend to be excellent prospects for coupons. The fact that the percentage of consumers identified as switchers has increased during recent years may, in fact, partially account for the rising usage of coupons by manufacturers.

Consumers who switch from one brand to another depending on which seems to be the best value at the time are very likely to be influenced by coupons, provided that they are coupon users. People

Exhibit 4.23.   Action Taken When Couponed Brand Isn't Found*

Go to another store	31%
Postpone purchase	27%
Discard coupon	19%
Buy a different brand	15%
Complain/speak to store manager	10%
Don't buy brand/do nothing	7%
Give coupon to someone else	3%

*Base = Coupon users
Multiple responses allowed.
Source: Courtesy of Manufacturers Coupon Control Center, Clinton, Iowa.

who have used a particular brand before may be persuaded to buy it again with a price incentive. And people who have never tried a particular brand, but who are not especially loyal to any one competitive brand, may use a coupon on a new brand, provided that the redemption value is sufficiently high. Insofar as coupons induce consumers to try new brands, they may ultimately add to long-term brand value by increasing the likelihood that those people may buy the brand in the future.

Consumers who are variety seekers may also be strongly affected by coupons, which may give them an extra incentive to buy a specific brand. Coupons are not likely to increase long-term brand value very much with variety seekers, however, since these consumers gain utility by using a variety of different products. Marketers of brands in categories where variety is a benefit tend to cross-ruff when using in-pack and on-pack coupons; for instance, General Mills may place a coupon for its Crispy Wheats 'n' Raisins in boxes of Wheaties.

Coupons may also be of some help in gaining or maintaining distribution for new or low-selling brands. Coupons may increase demand for certain brands at the retail level; in addition, retailers may fear that if consumers fail to find a couponed brand in the store, they may shop at another store for it.

Price Buyers

Consumers who look only at price may be persuaded to buy through the use of coupons if the value of the coupon is high enough to bring the price of the product below that of its competitors. However, without the coupon in the future, these consumers are likely to go back to purchasing whichever other brand is the most inexpensive.

Nonusers

Coupons generally do very little to persuade nonusers in a particular category to make a purchase. The rare exception may be when consumers are persuaded by a high-value coupon to purchase a brand; in that case, if they like the brand and use it again in the future, long-term value may have been created. This probably occurs very rarely, however.

Coupons can often be very successful in creating long-term value for a brand. They may persuade people who do not currently use a particular brand to try it; if those consumers like it, they may purchase it again in the future. In addition, couponing may help brands to obtain or maintain distribution, which can also result in long-term sales.

The Residual Value of Coupons

The difficult part of creating residual value with coupons, however, is in reaching the right consumers with the right offer. The most commonly cited problem in couponing is that discounts large enough to convince competitive users to try the brand are likely to be used to an even greater extent by loyals who very well might have purchased the brand anyway.

Because of this issue, marketers must make very clear decisions in advance about the goals they want to achieve with their couponing programs. Marketers who are using high-value coupons to prompt trial by new users generally need to resign themselves to sacrificing profits (or, at best, breaking even), due to redemptions by current customers who would have purchased the brand anyway. On the other hand, marketers may generate a sales spike and make a profit by distributing a coupon with a relatively low value, but this should not be assumed to create many new customers or add much long-term value.

New forms of distribution such as direct-mail and electronic couponing have the potential of addressing this issue, but their implementation has by and large been slow to develop. Although many packaged-goods manufacturers are examining using database marketing to address this problem, most are still investing relatively few resources in this area.

Chapter Five

Special Packs

Bonus packs, in-packs, on-packs, near-packs, and specialty containers are all similar in that they give the consumer something extra at the point of purchase. As such, they can be useful in creating impulse purchases, thereby increasing sales. In addition, some of these promotions may be successful in certain situations in increasing the long-term value of brands.

Types of Special Packs

Bonus Packs

The bonus pack normally consists of a special container, package, carton, or other holder in which the consumer is given more of the product than usual for the same price or perhaps even a lower price. The idea of the bonus pack is similar to that of the "baker's dozen," in which 13 items (such as doughnuts) are sold for the price of 12.

Exhibit 5.1. Bonus Pack: Larger Container
Source: Used by permission of H. J. Heinz Company.

Exhibit 5.2.   Bonus Pack: Extra Unit
Source: Courtesy of Armour-Dial, Inc. © 1980 Armour-Dial, Inc.

Bonus packs may consist either of a larger container filled with extra product (for instance, a ketchup bottle with six extra ounces) or of a group of several items sold together for a special price (for instance, four bars of soap banded together and sold for the price of three).

Bonus packs are usually limited to products that are fairly low in cost, that have high velocity (that is, are used up quickly), and in

Exhibit 5.3. Bonus Pack: Bic

Source: Photo courtesy of Bic Pen Corporation.

which additional product is a desirable reward in the eyes of the consumer.

Bonus packs are often used as an attempt to either reward or retain present customers and to take them out of the market for a longer period of time after the purchase, a ploy that is likely to be effective preceding periods when competitors are expected to be promoting. They can also be a successful way of getting attention at the point of purchase among parity products, and they are a sound way of presenting a price reduction to the consumer. Also, with the bonus pack, the manufacturer can be relatively sure that the "extra" product will reach the consumer rather than be absorbed as additional margin by the retailer.

The downside of bonus packs is that they can be expensive to implement. Although the cost of the additional product is often small, the new packaging and special handling required may be quite expensive. Retailers may also dislike bonus packs, especially if they are too large to fit in the space regularly allotted to the product in the store or warehouse; in some cases retailers may even refuse to carry them.

Bonus packs are generally unappealing to consumers who don't usually buy the product (the feeling is "If I don't usually use Brand X, why would I want two instead of one?"), and they do little to enhance brand value. Consumers may, in many cases, not believe that they are really getting extra product for their money, suspecting instead that the product is actually being sold at regular price.

In addition, manufacturers should be aware that retailers may sometimes remove banding and sell products separately. It therefore may be wise to make this difficult to do (for instance, by gluing the packages together rather than just using a paper band, or by labeling each item with a notation that it is part of a larger package and is not to be sold separately.

In-Packs and On-Packs

In-packs and on-packs both give consumers some sort of an immediate reward (other than extra product or price discount) for purchasing a brand. The premium is generally an item that is likely to be attractive to the targeted consumer, or it may be another product that the manufacturer would like the consumer to sample.

In-pack premiums are placed inside the package and may be anything from the "Toy Surprise" found inside boxes of Cracker Jack to towels, sheets, or dishes that once were found inside detergent boxes. This type of premium, for instance, is often found in

Exhibit 5.4.   In-Pack Premium
Source: Cracker Jack® is the trademark of Borden, Inc., for candied popcorn and peanuts.

the children's segment of the ready-to-eat breakfast cereal category, since the promise of a small toy is generally attractive to youngsters.

An on-pack is a premium attached to the product or product package in some way. For example, it might be banded to the product, attached to the product with a paper or rubber band, or blister-packed. Often the product and the on-pack premium are related—shaving creams with razors, canned cat food with plastic can covers, spices with recipe books. Premiums may also be less-popular products or new products sold by the same manufacturer that are distributed as on-packs as a way to get trial.

Exhibit 5.5.   In-Pack Premium: Cap'n Crunch Cereal
Source: Courtesy of Quaker Oats Company.

Although in-packs and on-packs are usually sold at the regular price of the product, there may be situations where a particularly attractive premium will allow the price to be raised to cover some of the additional cost.

In-packs and on-packs may differentiate the product at the point of sale, and they may be used to appeal to a specific segment of the

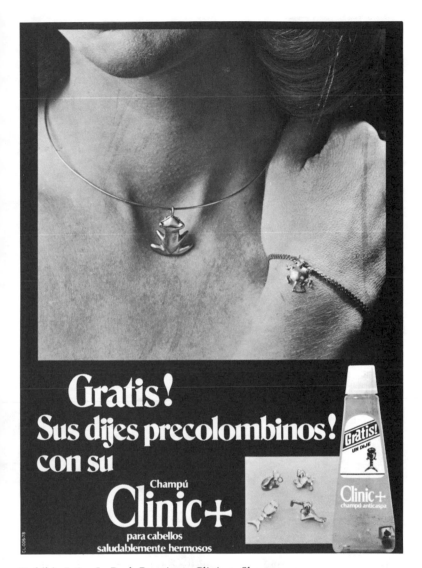

Exhibit 5.6.   In-Pack Premium: Clinic+ Shampoo
Source: William A. Robinson, *100 Best Sales Promotions* (Chicago: Crain Books, 1980), p. 133.

population. In addition, certain premiums may increase usage by reminding the consumer of the brand. For example, recipe books may encourage use of specialty foods such as cardamom or other spices; soup bowls may provide reminders for a particular brand of soup; and coffee mugs may increase coffee consumption.

In-pack and on-pack promotions may also be attractive to some marketers in that the cost of the promotion may be determined in

Exhibit 5.7.   On-Pack Premium: Gillette Shaving Cream
Source: Courtesy of The Gillette Company.

advance. Because the manufacturer can decide how many special packages will be produced and shipped, that number may be increased or decreased to conform to budgetary constraints.

In-packs and on-packs have many of the same negatives as bonus packs, however. They can be expensive to manufacture and distribute, and they may be refused by retailers if they don't fit in assigned spaces on store shelves or in the warehouse. Pretesting can be expensive, since it involves setting up the production lines to create the special products. If the premium is very attractive and is not securely packaged, theft or pilferage by consumers or store personnel may be a problem. Finally, some consumers who don't want the premium may decide not to buy the product at all, especially if the premium increases the price of the product.

Marketers who place in-packs inside food items also need to be aware of FDA regulations covering the types of materials that may be used.

Exhibit 5.8. Near-Pack Premium: Freshlike Frozen Vegetables
Source: Courtesy of The Larsen Company.

Near-Packs

The near-pack is offered free, or for an additional charge, with the product at the point of purchase. (When there is an extra charge involved, it may be called a *salable* or *price-plus pack*.)

Near-packs may be used because a premium is too large or too inconvenient to be attached to the regular product; the bulkiness of the premium may therefore lend itself to a display. For example,

Lever Brothers, working with the Marvel Comic Group, once developed a special near-pack Spiderman comic book to be given away with Aim toothpaste. The comic book focused on proper dental care as a storyline, and it was displayed in the toothpaste section of retail stores.

Near-packs have often been used at the retail level to generate store traffic. For instance, Burger King may give away drinking glasses to consumers purchasing certain menu items; gas stations may give away bottles of Coca-Cola or hats promoting NFL teams to drivers filling up their gas tanks; and supermarkets may give away dishes or encyclopedia volumes to consumers buying a certain dollar amount of groceries.

Like in-packs and on-packs, near-packs may be successful at generating interest in a dull product category. In addition, if the items are part of a series (for example, "Collect all six 'Star Wars' figures"), they can generate repeat purchases as consumers strive to collect the whole set. Near-packs are very flexible, and they may get displays for packaged goods into retail outlets that choose to accept them. Near-packs may also be useful in generating trial for other items in a product line—for instance, many cosmetic companies offer "bonus days" where purchasers of one item at the regular price can receive a special collection of lipsticks, moisturizers, perfumes, or other items either free or at a low price.

However, many retailers dislike near-packs (except for the ones that they themselves use to lure consumers into the store), as they believe that they can be a lot of trouble to stock, handle, display, and monitor. Near-packs may also sometimes compete with other products that the retailer sells (for instance, a lawnmower manufacturer that gives away hedge clippers with purchases may find that many of its retailers also sell hedge clippers), which could result in lower overall retail profits for the retailer if consumers don't have to buy the items being offered as premiums. Therefore manufacturers may not be able to get as many stores to agree to carry near-packs as they might like.

In addition, manufacturers that use near-packs also face the possibility that retailers may not display them properly or that the premiums may be stolen by retail employees or by consumers. For these reasons, near-packs are often restricted to situations where the marketer of the product has control over the handling of the premiums, such as when the manufacturer operates or controls retail stores (as is the case with fast-food outlets and gas stations) or when distribution can be controlled by marketer-employed personnel (such as at department store cosmetic counters).

Exhibit 5.9. Reusable Container: Paul Masson Wine

Source: Courtesy of Paul Masson Wine.

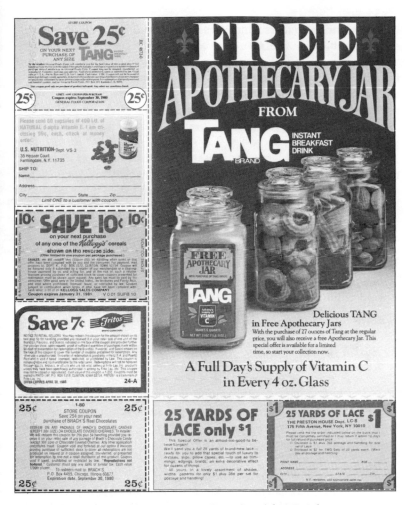

Exhibit 5.10. Reusable Container: Tang Breakfast Drink
Source: Courtesy of General Foods Corp.

Reusable Containers

A specialty container provides the consumer with a premium that can continue to be used after the product it holds is consumed. The most common premium of this type is the once-popular "jelly glass" that still graces many homes in the United States. Another example is Libby's tomato juice, which has been packed in a reusable decanter. The product might carry the regular price, or, if the container is very attractive, the price of the product may be increased to cover part or all of the cost of the container.

In addition to increasing sales of the product at the retail level, some reusable containers, such as coffee carafes, can encourage consumers to use the product more frequently in the future. (It is questionable, however, whether this will increase consumption for a particular brand rather than for all brands in the category.) Also, because specialty containers replace the regular packaging, that cost can be added to the value of the premium, allowing a better offer to be made.

The major problem with reusable containers is that if they are not the same size as the regular container or if they are fragile, they may present problems in handling, storing, and shelving at the retail level. Also, reusable containers that are unattractive to the consumer may actually result in decreased sales, particularly if they increase the price of the product.

Strategic Uses of Special Packs

Depending on the individual situation and how they are used, in-store premiums can be successful at gaining sales among a variety of consumers and, sometimes, at increasing future sales.

Loyal Users

Current customers are probably the most likely to be affected by these types of "value-added" promotions. Bonus packs are very effective at loading loyal users with extra product, at once taking them out of the market for other brands (thereby providing a defense during periods when other products are likely to be promoting) and (with impulse products such as cookies) increasing consumption after purchase. Bonus packs, in-packs, on-packs, near-packs, and reusable containers can also make consumers more likely to buy the products at the retail level; this can either encourage additional usage or change purchase timing by getting consumers to stock up.

Certain kinds of premiums (such as the Good Seasons salad dressing cruet) may also encourage more frequent usage of the product. And when in-pack, on-pack, or near-pack premiums consist of other products also sold individually by the same company, they can encourage crossover sales in the future among new customers who try and like them.

Competitive Loyals

Consumers who are intensely loyal to competitive products are unlikely to be swayed by value-added promotions such as the ones described in this chapter. If consumers do not want a particular product to begin with, they certainly will not be swayed by the opportunity to get more of it in a bonus pack. And although these consumers might want to obtain the premium offered in an in-pack, on-pack, near-pack, or specialty package, it is unlikely that they will buy a product they don't like in order to obtain it.

Consumers who are brand loyal to a competitive product because they think it's a slightly better deal, or because of inertia, may sometimes be influenced by an attractive premium. (Bonus packs usually work less well for these people.) For instance, a consumer who usually buys Amoco gasoline may decide to try Shell instead in order to pick up a stuffed animal for the kids. If this occurs, it is possible that the consumer will like the brand (or get used to using it) and will continue to buy it after the promotion is over.

However, it should be noted that in order to persuade any competitive loyal, even one who purchases out of inertia, to buy another brand, a very attractive premium offer must be made. Many in-store premiums are therefore ignored by competitive loyals much of the time.

Switchers

Premium offers such as bonus packs, near-packs, in-packs, on-packs, and reusable containers can be very strong incentives to switchers, who may be easily influenced by the extra push that these kinds of items bring to the product. In categories where variety seeking is an issue, it sometimes may be helpful to include a sample of a similar product as the premium, in the hope that the next time the consumer switches it will be to that brand rather than to a competitive brand.

The one big negative associated with many in-packs, on-packs, near-packs, and specialty packages is the distribution issue. Because many retailers dislike the hassles involved with in-store premium offers, they often refuse to carry them. This may mean that premium offers actually decrease distribution of the product. It is for this reason, and because of the increasing lack of power that manufacturers have over their distribution channels, that fewer companies offer premiums today than did in the past.

Price Buyers

Consumers who consistently buy the cheapest brand on the market will take advantage of a premium offer only if it is for an item that is of exceptional interest to them or if the price of the brand is substantially lowered. As with all promotions directed at price buyers, in-store premium offers should be expected to have little long-term value on the success of the brand.

Nonusers

Nonusers of a product category are even less likely to be influenced by premium offers than are competitive loyals. They certainly will not be swayed by the possibility of getting a larger amount of a type of product they never use, and they are also unlikely to be swayed by items offered through on-packs, in-packs, near-packs, and specialty packaging. Only if the premium is extremely attractive or not easily obtainable through other means, and if they already have some small interest in the product, are they likely to be influenced. For instance, it is conceivable that a person who never eats fast food might pick up a hamburger to obtain a poster from a special movie; however, this type of situation is likely to happen relatively infrequently and probably won't create much increased business after the promotion is over.

Special Packs and Residual Market Value

Bonus packs, in-packs, on-packs, near-packs, and reusable containers all make products more appealing to consumers. They appear to "reward" them for their purchases, thereby possibly generating positive feelings that may have some impact in the future. In addition, depending on what is being offered, premiums may cause people who don't usually buy or never buy a brand to try it; once this occurs, those people may be more likely to buy the brand in the future.

Some premiums may also encourage consumers to use more product in the future (or make it easier for them to do so); other premiums may remind consumers of the brand or (when the premium is a T-shirt or other frequently displayed item featuring the product name) turn them into walking billboards for it. Finally, cross-ruffed premiums that consist of samples of other products made by the same manufacturer may cause people to try those brands, which may result in future demand for them.

Chapter Six

Continuity Programs

Continuity programs are basically designed to create and reward brand loyalty among consumers who might otherwise switch from brand to brand within a category. They are especially popular in categories where consumer perception of product differentiation is low—a description that might apply to products as expensive as airline flights and as pedestrian as corn flakes.

Frequent-buyer programs are one of the fastest-growing forms of consumer promotion. Spending on continuity programs was approximately $1.6 billion in 1989.[1]

In continuity plans, consumers are rewarded for making multiple purchases of a particular product or service. Usually, continuity offers are made over fairly long periods of time, since the consumer usually has to make several purchases (or, in the case of a retail store, visits) in order to collect the premium or gain the reward.

A major difference between continuity programs and other forms of sales promotion is the time lag between the product purchase and the receipt of the reward or gift. Unlike most sales promotion programs, where gratification is immediate, continuity programs require consumers to wait before they receive the desired item. Moreover, the eventual rewards from continuity programs tend to be much larger than those found in other types of sales promotions.

Types of Continuity Programs

Continuity programs have become important tools for doing business in certain service industries, such as airlines (most now have some sort of frequent-flyer program) and hotels (with chains such as Hyatt now offering frequent-guest programs). These programs have been successful in providing consumers with an extra benefit in categories in which all brands generally offer similar prices and

---

[1] *The Premium/Incentive Business' Annual Industry Survey*, 1990.

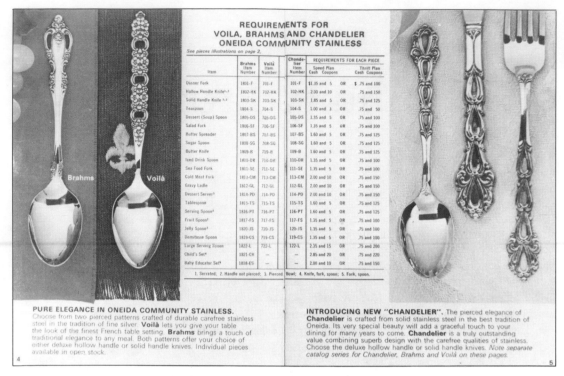

Exhibit 6.1.   Continuity Coupons
Source: Courtesy of General Mills, Inc.

service levels. They have been especially popular with consumers who travel often on business (the largest and most profitable segment of the travel industry), largely because these people are able to use the rewards from the program for their own personal or vacation travel.

Frequent-traveler programs run by airlines, hotels, rental car agencies, and other businesses generally give out a certain number of "points" for miles flown or visits made; these can then be exchanged for free services or upgrades in the future. A new twist on frequent-traveler programs is that certain credit card or travel card companies now offer points on various companies' frequent-user programs for purchases charged on the card—making it possible, for instance, to become a "frequent flyer" without ever leaving the ground. Frequent-traveler clubs often offer special benefits to very frequent purchasers, such as automatic upgrades to first class and the ability to accumulate benefits more quickly than other, less-valued customers.

Spurred on by the success of frequent-traveler industries, many other kinds of businesses have begun using databases to establish

Guinness Book of World Records
FREE! (MAIL 2 INNER SEALS FROM NESCAFÉ INSTANT COFFEE~EXCEPT THE 2-OZ. SIZE)

OVER 2,000 NEW ENTRIES!

The Guinness Book of World Records is the famous encyclopedia of all the records set by man and Mother Nature, from the world's tallest man (8 feet, 11.1 inches) to the world's longest sermon (over 48 hours) to the world's shortest river (440 feet at low tide).

And now you can get the Guinness Book of World Records FREE, just by filling out the order blank and sending it in with two inner seals from Nescafé.

The World's Longest Moustache.
An Indian Brahmin sports a record moustache 102 inches long. It took 13 years to grow, and costs over $30.00 a year to keep up.

The World's Oldest Goldfish.
One old fish story is really true! Although goldfish rarely live more than 17 years, the world's oldest goldfish celebrated its 40th birthday.

The World's Worst Tongue-Twister.

"The Sixth Sick Sheik's Sixth Sheep's Sick."

The World's Largest Selling Brand of Instant Coffees—Nescafé.
Nescafé is the world's leading brand of instant coffees because Nescafé has the kind of flavor the world likes best. You can save 40¢ on your next jar of Nescafé Instant Coffee, any size—Regular or Decaffeinated. Clip your 40¢ coupon now and redeem it at your food store. And be sure to save the inner seals from Nescafé for your free copy of the Guinness Book of World Records.

To get your FREE copy of the Guinness Book of World Records (over $2.00 value):
Mail this order blank, together with 2 inner seals from Nescafé (except 2-oz.) and your name and address to **World Record Book Offer, P.O. Box 1715, Maple Plain, Minn. 55348**

NAME
ADDRESS
CITY   STATE   ZIP

STORE COUPON
SAVE 40¢
on any size jar of Nescafé Instant Coffee, Regular or Decaffeinated.
EXPIRES AUGUST 31, 1977

Exhibit 6.2. Limited-Time Continuity Plan
Source: William A. Robinson, *100 Best Sales Promotions of 1977/78* (Chicago: Crain Books, 1979), p. 110.

their own frequent-buyer clubs. Waldenbooks (its sales threatened in many markets by discount-priced rivals) began a program where, for a small initial fee, members were entitled to automatic discounts on merchandise and received store credits through the mail for every $100 spent. A side benefit of the program is that the chain was able to develop a list of its customers and their buying behaviors, which could be useful in future marketing efforts.

Credit card companies have also initiated continuity plans for their cardholders by offering "bonus points" that can be applied to discounted merchandise to customers charging purchases on their cards. For each purchase, the Book-of-the-Month Club offers points that can be applied toward the purchase of older titles that are overstocked.

Other retailers, such as grocery stores, also frequently offer continuity programs. A decade or two ago, these continuity programs centered around trading stamps, such as S&H Green Stamps. Consumers who collected stamps could trade them for merchandise displayed in catalogs or catalog stores.

Although trading stamps are less popular than they once were, retailers still often use continuity programs to keep customers coming into their stores rather than competitors'. For instance, many food stores offer a free turkey at Thanksgiving or Christmas in exchange for a certain amount in cash register receipts. Another popular retailer program is offering a series of items to consumers, each of which must be acquired individually on different shopping occasions. For example, consumers may obtain a new volume in a cookbook set, or a new pan in a set of cookware, each week they shop at a particular supermarket. Obviously, these programs are designed to keep consumers returning to the store in order to obtain the complete set of items.

Other merchants, such as florists, coffee shops, and restaurants, have also offered continuity programs, which give free or reduced-price merchandise to "Frequent Flower Buyers," "Frequent Sippers," or "Frequent Diners."

Continuity programs have been less successful for packaged-goods products, for a number of reasons. For one thing, manufacturers usually do not have direct contact with their customers, and it therefore can be difficult to get them to sign up for a program. Also, because packaged-goods products tend to have low value and low manufacturer margins, it may be necessary to require the consumer to make an extremely large number of purchases before any premium of real value can be acquired.

Nevertheless, some manufacturers have been successful in incorporating continuity elements into sales promotion programs. For

Exhibit 6.3. Store Continuity Program
Source: Courtesy of Jewel Food Stores.

instance, some through-the-mail premiums require that consumers submit several proofs of purchase to obtain free merchandise through the mail. (Because these plans have a limited duration, however, they are usually not considered to be true continuity programs encouraging long-term brand loyalty.)

Manufacturers have also occasionally used in-pack or on-pack premiums as a method of running continuity programs. For instance, Breeze detergent at one time included towels and washcloths inside packages of its detergent, in the hope that consumers would repeatedly purchase the product in order to obtain a complete set.

Continuity programs do have drawbacks, however, in that they train consumers to be brand loyal only on the basis of the rewards rather than because of the product itself. In some cases the programs may even cause consumers to wonder about the merits of the product. For instance, when consumers bought Breeze, it probably was unclear to them whether they bought it because they liked the prod-

Exhibit 6.4. Continuity Game Program
Source: Eugene Mahany, "Promo Techniques Spread Wings," *Advertising Age,* April 28, 1980, p. 60.

uct or because of the towels. Once the towels were no longer being given away, or once consumers had enough towels and didn't want any more, it was questionable whether they would continue to buy the brand.

This problem has been apparent even in the airline industry, where continuity programs have become an important element in doing business. Some marketing managers, for instance, believe that because all airlines offer basically the same programs to their members, frequent-flyer clubs have ceased to be a differentiating factor and instead are now a cost of doing business.

Another problem with continuity plans is that they may create large liabilities for companies that use accounting methods requiring them to treat all benefits of such programs as though they will actually be cashed in. For this reason, some companies using continuity programs have instituted expiration dates on the use of the benefits, thereby reducing permanent liabilities in the programs.

Continuity programs can be successful in increasing loyalty for a particular product, especially in situations where real differences between products are slight. Continuity programs take consumers out of the market for competitive products to a large extent, and they may in some cases make consumers more excited about the product being purchased. They can also be successful at giving the marketer a list of the company's most valued customers; these people then may be targeted with intensive selling messages later.

However, continuity programs also have many disadvantages. They must run for a long period of time, meaning that they require a big commitment on the part of the marketer. Consumers must also make a big commitment if they are going to get the rewards of the program, and they may become impatient while waiting to obtain the desired items. Continuity programs are also unlikely to be effective for inexpensive or infrequently purchased products, since the lag time before an attractive reward can be given is likely to be unrealistically long.

Because continuity programs require a major investment in time and money, it can be helpful for manufacturers to consult a professional organization that specializes in this field. Usually, such programs are fairly complex, require a great deal of handling, and can be quite risky if not properly planned. Here are some general areas that should be given particular attention:

Planning Continuity Programs

1. *Objectives of the continuity program.* Will the program run for a short period of time and offer a number of coupons or proofs of purchase for obtaining one specific item, or will it be an ongoing program in which several prizes or gifts are available over time? Each has a different set of objectives, costs, and sales promotion implementations.

2. *Type of proof of purchase or coupon required.* Some products or packages lend themselves to easily providing a proof of purchase or label, and in some situations, such as the airline industry, the company itself may keep track of the purchases. In other cases, however, obtaining a proof of purchase is not so simple. For instance, getting a proof of purchase from a plastic or metal container is sometimes nearly impossible.

Exhibit 6.5. · Continuity Program: Post Cereal
Source: William A. Robinson, *100 Best Sales Promotions of 1976/77* (Chicago: Crain Books, 1977), p. 27.

3. *Number and cost of premiums.* This is obviously a key element in the success of any continuity program. If the prize structure is limited to one item, has it been pretested for consumer acceptance? A program offering a prize or gift with little or no appeal is usually

worse than no program at all. What will be the cost of the premium? Based on the selling price of the product, is it affordable? Finally, what about the availability of prizes? Nothing upsets consumers more than to save for a gift and then find that it's not available.

4. *Structure of the program.* Will only proofs of purchase be accepted, or may cash be substituted for some of them? If the premium is to be packed in the product, will this create problems with production or distribution?

5. *Duration of the offer.* The time period of the offer must be long enough so that the average consumer will be able to make sufficient purchases to obtain the gift. If there is no initial time limit, there will be consumer resistance if an attempt is made to institute a deadline later on.

6. *Handling the fulfillment of the offer.* How will the prize or gift be distributed—through stores, through the mail? Who is to accept the orders, check them, and distribute the premiums?

All of the above questions and many others must be answered in the process of setting up a continuity plan. Therefore it can often be helpful to contact organizations specializing in these kinds of activities.

Strategic Uses of Continuity Programs

As previously stated, a continuity program can be successful in building brand loyalty during the length of the promotion and in warding off competitive threats. The main issues with this kind of program are in finding rewards that will be attractive to consumers and that will correspond to budgetary constraints, and in getting consumers to begin and to continue to participate in the program.

Loyal Users

Continuity programs are often helpful in allowing companies to capitalize on their current customers. Loyal users are relatively likely to enroll in a continuity program, since they usually purchase the brand anyway; once enrolled, they become even less likely to be lured away by competitors' promotional activities.

Also, in certain situations consumers may be tempted to buy more of a particular product in order to gain points that bring them closer to a reward, or to obtain a certain desired item in a series promotion. Finally, in situations where a number of products are tied together into one continuity program, crossover sales may occur as users of one type of product try others in order to obtain points to be used toward getting the prize. If that occurs and if consumers like the products they sample, then they may continue to buy them even after the promotion is over.

Competitive Loyals

Continuity programs are much less effective in addressing competitive loyals than are most sales promotion programs. Most competitive loyals will be unwilling to make a commitment to buying another brand on a regular basis. Only those consumers who are loyal, mostly because of inertia, and who are attracted by a particularly good reward are likely to even consider participating in a continuity program.

Switchers

Switchers are very good targets for continuity programs. Because continuity programs provide a point of differentiation to the consumer, they may often succeed in creating brand loyalty to a particular product. Although some switchers may get used to using a particular product and continue to do so even after the promotion is over, most of this increased brand loyalty will last only until the continuity program is over.

Switchers who use different brands because they enjoy the variety, however, are unlikely to commit themselves to a continuity program. It may be for this reason that continuity programs are used in few categories where variety is a motivator.

Price Buyers

Unless the reward is particularly desirable, price buyers are unlikely to be tempted by continuity programs, since getting a good deal on the purchase price is usually a more important motivator to these people than obtaining a free gift sometime in the future. Only if the price is competitive and rewards are large will they be likely to commit to a program.

Nonusers

Continuity programs are unlikely to have any effect on nonusers of the product category. If people are not using any product in the category, then they are unlikely to anticipate that they will start using it often enough in the future to obtain the reward, no matter how attractive it might be.

In certain circumstances continuity programs can be very effective in reducing switching and getting consumers to stick with a particular brand. However, whether they actually have any effect on brand equity—that is, on consumers' perception of the brand and on their willingness to buy the product after the continuity program is over— is often doubtful.

Continuity programs usually do not make consumers more aware of the inherent benefits of a brand; instead, they offer a reward (or "bribe") to get consumers to buy the product over an extended period of time. One problem with this is that if the continuity program is successful, it may be easily matched by other companies, with the result that profit margins will, in effect, be lowered throughout the industry. In addition, consumers easily get used to obtaining the rewards of continuity programs, meaning that the programs can be extremely difficult to discontinue. In many cases, too, continuity programs can distract attention from such "real" category benefits as service or product quality, meaning that in the long run they can result in consumers who buy only because of price or "deals."

In some cases, however, continuity programs have the potential of helping marketers learn more about their customers and market to them more effectively. For instance, Waldenbooks' frequent-reader club allows the company to keep track of individuals' purchases; this information can then be used by Waldenbooks to sell other products to these customers. As an example, frequent buyers of cookbooks enrolled in Waldenbooks' club might be sent a special newsletter describing in detail new cookbooks on the market; they might also be invited to attend a special seminar hosted by the author of a new cookbook. Although most marketers offering continuity programs have only begun to use information in this way, these types of promotions have the potential of providing the consumer with a real added benefit related to the product (thereby improving consumer perception of the company), and of increasing volume among segments of consumers.

Continuity programs may often be most advantageous to the larger firms in the industry. When consumers are forced to choose between competing companies' programs, they often may choose the brand that seems most convenient (for instance, the airline with the most flights, the hotel chain with the most locations, or the bookstore located closest to home), or, in the case of packaged goods, the brand they already use most often (which will usually be the brand with the biggest market share). This may mean that, if all competitors in an industry institute continuity programs, some switchers may altogether cease purchasing products or services from

Continuity Programs and Residual Value

the smaller players. Therefore the smaller marketers in an industry should usually think long and hard before they begin continuity programs, even if those programs seem advantageous in the short run.

In fact, because of the issues involved, all marketers who are considering instituting continuity programs need to think carefully about what they are hoping to accomplish and about whether they are willing to commit to the program for the long term. Companies that are simply hoping to perk up short-term profits should probably look to other types of promotions to accomplish that goal.

Chapter Seven

Refunds

In a way, refunds can be viewed as coupons that offer delayed gratification to the consumer. Refund offers generally allow consumers to buy a product and then, through the mail, get back a portion of the purchase price.

However, while the popularity of coupons has grown dramatically over the last decade or so, the usage of rebates has been generally flat. Rebates may be less appealing to some consumers who want immediate gratification, and rising postage costs have made refunds less attractive to both the consumer and the manufacturer.

Uses of Refunds

A refund (or rebate) is simply an offer by a manufacturer to return to the consumer a certain amount of money when a particular product or group of products is purchased.

Although refund offers originated in the food business, they are often used today on more expensive items, such as over-the-counter drugs, electronics, health-care and beauty-care products, liquor, appliances, and automobiles. Refunds have been especially popular on these types of products because they enable the manufacturer to deliver to the consumer a substantial discount without the major misredemption problems that can often accompany the use of high-value coupons.

Although refunds are still used occasionally on low-priced products, there are several reasons why they are used less often. First, postage rates have increased rapidly, meaning that a refund of 50 cents or $1 is likely to be perceived as not worthwhile by both the consumer (who must mail in a proof of purchase with a request for the refund) and by the manufacturer (who must mail back checks to consumers). In addition, many consumers today have become brand switchers and are less likely to be willing to purchase eight tubes of toothpaste to acquire a $2 refund. Finally, because manufacturer margins are low on most grocery items, it is difficult to make an attractive offer.

High-value refunds may occasionally be used effectively, however, on new packaged-goods products or on brands with low market share. They may also be effective on products being moved into new geographic areas or by companies developing new patterns of distribution.

Refunds may also be used effectively on brands that are priced higher than the competition, in order to induce trial without a price cut. For example, Bailey's Irish Cream liqueur, a premium brand in the category, once used a rebate to get first-time buyers of Irish creams to sample Bailey's rather than a competitive product.

Since refunds tend to be most attractive when they are for relatively large amounts of money, they are particularly effective in generating trial for fairly expensive, high-margin products that are purchased frequently by consumers, such as batteries, pet food, or liquor. Because these products are expensive, a large rebate may be offered; because they are purchased frequently, consumers may decide they like the brand and purchase it in the future.

Refunds may also be effective in getting consumers to buy slow-moving, parity-type, impulse products that are often used up quickly once they are purchased. They also work well in product categories in which there is not a constant barrage of sales promotion activities or media advertising.

Refunds are often used by manufacturers because they attract attention to brands at the point of purchase at relatively low expense. There is evidence to suggest that consumers who take advantage of refund offers may be better able to remember the brand than with other offers. In addition, manufacturers may benefit from slippage, which occurs when consumers buy the product and plan to take advantage of the rebate but neglect to send for it. Slippage rates with refund offers may be considerable, averaging 20 percent in the grocery products category.

In cases where more than one purchase must be made to get the refund, this type of sales promotion can load some consumers with product, making it more difficult for competitors to make immediate sales and sometimes getting consumers accustomed to purchasing a particular brand. Products flagged with refund offers may also attract attention at the point of purchase and may occasionally help to get in-store displays for brands.

Another advantage of refunds is that they may sometimes prompt response from consumers who are not affected by coupons. According to Manufacturer's Coupon Control Center, 44 percent of nonusers of coupons claim to have sent in a proof of purchase in order to obtain a refund check. And because refunds require consumers to supply their names and addresses, this type of promotion can be helpful to companies wishing to establish customer databases.

As previously mentioned, however, refunds have a number of disadvantages. Rising postage costs have made it less worthwhile for consumers to submit their proofs of purchase and for companies to mail checks to consumers. Busy consumers may be turned off by the trouble of mailing in their requests for refunds and by the need to purchase more than one item; they may also be discouraged by the need to wait weeks for the refund to arrive. Some consumers may submit proofs of purchase from items bought before the refund offer, meaning that the company can end up giving discounts on items that have already been sold.

In short, although refunds can be appropriate for some products and some situations, their effects on sales are usually much less observable than those of coupons.

Types of Refunds

Refunds may be offered on a single purchase of a product or on a number of purchases. Increasingly, though, manufacturers are structuring their rebate programs so that only one purchase needs to be made to obtain the rebate. This type of promotion addresses consumers' increasing desire for quick gratification, and it can result in higher response rates.

With low-priced products, such as groceries or health-care and beauty-care items, this strategy may mean that the entire purchase price (or most of it) must be refunded if the refund is to be large enough to be attractive to consumers. Obviously, companies that refund such a large amount are focused on the long term, and they are often trying to create trial for a new product in a competitive and (usually) high-margin category. In many cases, in fact, this kind of refund may act as a selective sampling program geared to consumers who, because they must go to the trouble of searching for the product and sending in for the refund, are more interested in the product category than is the rest of the population. Like most brand-building sales promotion activities, this type of refund offer works best for brands that are of equal or better quality or value compared to the competition and that previously have been used by a relatively small percentage of the population.

More expensive products, such as durable goods, have the luxury of offering rebates on single products even after the initial trial period, in order to attract consumer attention and provide a sales boost for the brand. In the case of high-priced items, such as automobiles, rebates may total $1,000 to $2,000 or more. More modestly,

Exhibit 7.1. Refund: Purchase of One Product
Source: William A. Robinson, *100 Best Sales Promotions* (Chicago: Crain Books, 1980), p. 115.

makers of some higher-priced packaged goods, such as Butterball turkeys, may pay $1 to $2 refunds in exchange for a single proof of purchase.

Refunds may also be made on multiple purchases of the same brand, although this kind of offer is less popular than in the past. This type of rebate generally fails to attract new customers to a particular product, since people are unlikely to risk purchasing several packages of a brand they haven't tried before.

Refunds made on multiple purchases of a brand tend to be used in categories where product is purchased often and brand loyalty is low, resulting in frequent switching. For instance, an orange juice manufacturer may offer a refund of $1 on six cans of frozen juice.

Occasionally a manufacturer may choose to tie several of its products together into a single rebate offer. This type of rebate may be more cost-efficient to distribute to the consumer, and it may help to give a boost to weaker products in the line; in addition, requiring

Exhibit 7.2. Refund Offer: Purchase of Several Products
Source: Courtesy of Beatrice Foods, Inc.

purchase of several products may allow a very attractive rebate to be made. However, this type of refund offer usually has a much lower response rate than other refund offers, because consumers may not be interested in purchasing all of the products being promoted. Therefore such a rebate often gives consumers a choice—for example, Procter & Gamble may link all of its personal products together in an offer that allows consumers to get $5 if they buy several items. Another way to make this type of offer attractive to a wide variety of consumers yet still obtain the advantages of a multiproduct offer

Exhibit 7.3. Refund Offer: Purchase of Paired Products
Source: Courtesy of Carr's© Crackers.

is to take a tiered approach: "Buy one of these items and get $1 back; buy both and get $3 back!"

Marketers may occasionally choose to run a refund offer with their own brand and another "related" product in order to attract consumer attention and suggest a use for the brand. Sometimes the related product may be a brand made by another manufacturer; in that case the two companies might split the cost of the promotion.

For instance, Hershey's chocolate, Keebler graham crackers, and Kraft marshmallows might team up in a refund program encouraging consumers to make S'Mores, a popular dessert sandwich. By encouraging expanded usage of the products, the promotion might result in increased sales at a fairly low cost for each of the three manufacturers.

Other promotions pair a particular product with a related generic item, such as Oreo cookies and vanilla ice cream. The idea here is either to suggest new usage ideas that may be repeated in the future or simply to promote trial of one product by giving consumers a "deal" on something that they would have had to purchase anyway. For instance, Carr's crackers, a high-quality, low-share brand, offered consumers a $2 refund when they purchased two packages of crackers and "your favorite cheese."

Cause-Related Refunds

Often, companies' work with charitable organizations is classified as public relations, since contributions are made out of a sense of corporate responsibility or to create public goodwill, rather than to generate sales.

In some cases, however, donations are tied to product purchases. For instance, a cereal manufacturer might donate 10 cents to the U.S. Olympic Team for every box of cereal sold. That type of program could in some ways be considered a refund offer, except that the money is donated to the not-for-profit organization rather than being returned to the consumer.

Sales promotions that tie charitable causes to purchases have become increasingly popular in recent years, probably because they combine some of the best features of public relations and sales promotion. Promotions of this type generate positive feelings among consumers, but they tend to be even better at this than straight charitable contributions in that they draw attention to the support of the cause and lead consumers to feel good about themselves (and therefore about the sponsoring organization) without having to contribute money out of their own pockets. In addition, in certain circumstances charitable programs can be very successful in encouraging consumers to buy a particular brand.

This kind of program can be very successful at persuading consumers to choose one product over another when it appears that there is little differentiation between the two and when price discounting by all the players has become common. For instance, U.S. Sprint has donated a percentage of its sales to the environment, to provide a point of differentiation in the competitive long-distance telephone service business. Dominick's, a supermarket chain in Chicago, offers local charitable organizations a chance to hold promotions where a small percentage of all sales to the group's supporters who identify themselves on a particular day is donated back to the group. (The promotions are generally successful not just at getting consumers into the store, but also at persuading them to stock up for the future.)

In categories where all the products appear to be basically the same, charitable promotions can sometimes be even more effective than price discounting. When consumers get a small price reduction, they may not consider it to be very significant. But the same amount donated to a good cause may make them feel positive about their purchase and focus not just on the individual donation from their own purchase but on the accumulated donations from all products sold. (For instance, the promise that "McDonald's will donate 5 percent of all sales to the 'Make a Wish Foundation' for terminally ill youngsters, or a minimum of $500,000" may appear to be much more attractive than an offer of "Ten cents off on all burgers!").

Although this type of promotion can be very successful at differentiating parity brands, it probably is less successful in categories where a large percentage of consumers have a clear preference for one of the products. In that case the small amount of personal satisfaction that consumers get from helping out a worthy cause will probably not outweigh their desire to be able to use the brand they like best. This kind of promotion also tends to be poor at luring nonusers to buy a particular type of product, since they are likely to believe that there are more efficient ways to donate to a worthy charity than to buy a product they don't need.

Cause-related promotions tend to be particularly effective when the organization to receive the donation is somehow connected to the company's consumer base. For instance, Ben & Jerry's, a super-premium ice cream that appeals to young, upscale, environmentally conscious consumers, donates money to preserve Brazilian rainforests. Nike, a sneaker brand popular in inner cities, supports educational programs targeted at African Americans. Levi Strauss, whose jeans are popular in the gay community, donates money to AIDS research.

Refunds and Other Sales Promotions

Refunds can often provide a nice boost to other types of sales promotion activities. For instance, coupons distributed to consumers may be accompanied by refund offers; the combination of the immediate and long-term incentives to purchase may prove to be very attractive. Another method is to send coupons to customers who have requested a rebate; this may help to reinforce the initial purchase and possibly

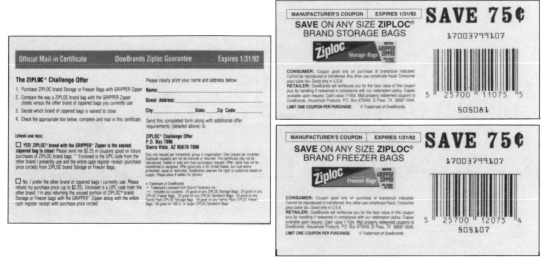

Exhibit 7.4. Refund and Coupons: Ziploc Offer
Source: Courtesy of DowBrands.

make the consumer more likely to buy the brand again in the future. ("Bounce-back" coupons of this type are usually very successful, sometimes achieving redemption rates of 80 percent or more.) In addition, if the coupon is mentioned in the original materials describing the refund offer, it may cause more people to respond.

Rebates may also be used effectively in conjunction with sweepstakes. Although consumers may not be required to make a purchase to enter a sweepstakes, some manufacturers have successfully structured their promotions so that consumers who mail in refund claims are entered automatically. This may increase the likelihood that consumers will actually buy the product rather than just sending in their names, as happens in many sweepstakes.

Another way that rebates may be used is as a "guarantee" to consumers who have not used the product before. Typically, consumers are offered a cash or check refund if they don't like the product, or the opportunity to obtain coupons for more product if they do like it. For instance, users of food storage bags were invited to judge how easy it was to close Ziploc bags compared to their regular brand. (See Exhibit 7–6.) Those who chose their original brand received $2.25 in cash; those picking Ziploc got an equal amount in coupons for future Ziploc purchases. (To make consumers more likely to request the coupon, however, and to make them more likely to tell themselves that the challenger is really better than their current brand, the value of the coupons is often set at a much

Exhibit 7.5.   Consumers Who Have Sent in for Refund

Consumers who have sent in proof of purchase to obtain a refund*

Type of refund requested	Coupon users	Non-users
Check	75%	44%
Cash	50%	22%
Bounceback coupon	50%	NA
Merchandise	34%	17%

*Base = Those respondents who have heard of refund offers
Source: Courtesy of Manufacturers Coupon Control Center, Clinton, Iowa.

greater amount than that of the cash.) In addition to generating trial, the Ziploc promotion encouraged consumers to actively notice and examine one of the brand's benefits, making it more likely that they will buy the product in the future.

Consumer Usage

Although all demographic groups tend to be aware of refund offers, and although many consumers who don't use coupons do occasionally take advantage of them, coupon users tend to be the heaviest users of rebates. Larger households, heavy coupon users, traditional single-income families, and women are also likely to be heavy users of refunds, according to the Manufacturer's Coupon Control Center.

Refund Offer Development

Refund offers are generally planned and carried out by sales promotion managers and departments, with the exception of the fulfillment of the offer (remitting the refund check or cash to the consumer).

Refund promotions themselves are usually not difficult to set up, and they can often be initiated rather quickly. However, since refund offers can be expensive and amounts being refunded can be quite large, a good system of control over the technique is a must. For example, computer software programs are available that ascertain that individuals obtain only one refund each and that proofs of purchase are valid.

A major factor in the success of a refund offer is the fulfillment procedure. Usually, this is best handled by a fulfillment organization that is set up to handle redemption programs. Typical costs for a refund offer fulfillment in 1990 were approximately $3.20 per thousand replies received. The marketer pays the fulfillment organization on the basis of the number of replies received and filled as a result of the promotion.

For example, assume a manufacturer offers a $2 refund for three proofs of purchase. The consumer sends the three proofs along with the refund offer form to the fulfillment organization, which checks to make certain that the requirements are met and mails the check or cash to the consumer. The fulfillment house then bills the advertiser for the actual orders filled; that is, if 20,000 orders are received, the fulfillment house bills the advertiser $64 ($3.20 per thousand × 20,000 responses). In most cases the fulfillment house would be responsible for the costs of the return card and the envelope and of addressing the refund. The postage might or might not be included, depending on the rate used. The marketer would, of course, also provide the fulfillment house with the $40,000 in refunds to be sent to the consumers.

One opportunity that marketers should not overlook is the ability to use fulfillment of the refund to further promote the product to the consumer. Too often, consumers receive rebate checks that state only the name of the fulfillment house, with no clue as to what product purchase actually prompted the refund payment. Since consumers are likely to feel positive about receiving a refund check, however, it is likely that if the sponsoring brand is named, some of that good feeling may rub off onto the product itself. Materials that might be included with the refund check include coupons for the same product or for other products made by the same manufacturer (especially appropriate since responders to refund offers are likely to use coupons) or a simple "Thank you" for the purchase.

Redemption

Traditionally, redemption of refund offers has been about 1 to 2 percent of the media circulation of the offer. For example, if the refund offer were made in newspapers with a combined circulation of 1,000,000, then refunds should not exceed 10,000 to 20,000.

Refund redemption rates do vary by media, however. Generally, the closer the offer is to the actual product, the higher the redemption rate—for example, on-pack refund offers do better than tear-off pads, which do better than media offers. However, it is not absolutely certain which of these techniques is best at creating new sales for the brand; it may be, for instance, that on-pack offers are more often noticed and used by people who would have purchased the product anyway.

Redemption rates can often be improved through the use of other promotional techniques. Media advertising, point-of-purchase materials, and, especially, "flags" on the front of the product itself can all cause more consumers to take advantage of the rebate offer.

Exhibit 7.6. Maximum Number of Proofs of Purchase

Maximum number of proofs of purchase consumers are willing to submit*	
All respondents	3.9
Coupon users	4.2
Non-users	3.0
Intensity of coupon use	
Light	3.5
Medium	4.0
Heavy	5.0
Household size	
1-2 members	3.4
3-4 members	4.2
5 or more members	5.1

*Base = Respondents who have sent in proof of purchase to obtain a refund.
Source: Courtesy of Manufacturers Coupon Control Center, Clinton, Iowa.

One of the major advantages of refund offers is their flexibility. The number of refunds made may be increased or decreased by varying three factors:

1. The value of the refund may be raised or lowered. If a refund of $2 is presently being used, activity can be increased by offering a $3 refund. Of course, lowering the refund value reduces redemptions.

2. The number of proofs of purchase required can be raised or lowered. By increasing the number, redemptions can be reduced. By lowering the requirements, the number of redemptions will increase.

3. By varying the ways the offer is advertised, the number of refunds can be increased or decreased.

Costs

In addition to the value of the refund itself, several other costs are incurred in a refund offer:

- Media advertising to support the offer.
- Point-of-purchase materials, order pads, or other display materials for use at retail.
- Handling fees by the fulfillment house: postage, envelopes, labor, and related costs.
- If a coupon is used, the clearinghouse fees for handling, plus the usual handling fee to the retailer.

To estimate the cost of a refund offer, manufacturers must first determine the actual costs involved, including additional handling or other fees, and then compare that number to the estimated return.

For example, assume that a marketer is making a purchase price refund on a package of rice that retails at 69 cents. In addition to the refund price of 69 cents, the fulfillment organization would charge the marketer approximately $3.00 for each 1,000 refunds received and returned, plus the cost of postage and supplies (such as envelopes and forms.)

Rules

Perhaps the most important factor in presenting the refund offer is making the rules clear. State clearly how many proofs of purchase are required. Tell exactly what will be accepted as a proof of purchase. Make the order blank clear and complete. In Exhibit 7–2 you'll find a sample of what we consider to be a good form for making the refund offer.

Other Guidelines

Manufacturers Marketing Services has developed the following checklist for marketers conducting refund offers:

- Keep the offer simple and give clear instructions.
- Require the standard proof of purchase—nothing esoteric.
- Require the respondent's zip code.
- Allow four weeks for delivery.
- Choose shorter expiration dates for media offers and longer ones for offers made on point-of-purchase materials and in-pack or on-pack.
- Put the expiration date in bold type and make it easy to find.
- Limit the refund offer to one per family.

Strategic Uses of Refunds

Obviously, some consumers never respond to any refund offer, whereas others respond to many offers. For consumers who are prone to respond to refund offers, however, the value of this kind of promotion can vary depending on the objectives that have been developed.

Loyal Users

Loyal users are the most likely consumers to take advantage of refund offers. Although refunds may make it even more likely that loyals may buy a particular product, however, it is questionable whether this will actually result in overall increased profits, especially since the values of many refunds tend to be quite large in comparison to the overall price of the product.

Certain refund offers may have a moderate effect on coaxing extra sales from current customers. One instance where this may work is in infrequently purchased, impulse-type items: a consumer who occasionally drinks single-malt Scotch may notice a refund offer on the bottle and decide to purchase it as a treat. Certainly, purchase timing may also be affected: A loyal driver of the Honda Accord may trade in for a new model a year earlier than planned if an attractive manufacturer rebate is offered.

Another situation where extra sales might be gained from current customers is in promotions where multiple purchases must be made in order to obtain the refund. The consumer might stock up on the product in order to be able to send in for the refund. This is likely to be most beneficial in categories where extra product purchased is easily consumed, such as ice cream. (Incidentally, if the extra product is *not* going to be quickly consumed, then it is necessary to make the proof of purchase easy to remove from the package. For example, if consumers must buy five boxes of facial tissue to obtain a refund, and they have to cut holes in the boxes before they're opened to get the proofs to send in, they are likely to be annoyed at both the process and the company.)

Some refund offers that link two products can be successful at getting loyal users of one product to try another product made by the same manufacturer. As mentioned earlier, however, this type of strategy may ultimately result in lower overall redemption rates.

Competitive Loyals

Like most sales promotion activities, refunds are unlikely to influence consumers who are intensely loyal to a competitive product. However, because they often offer consumers a fairly large discount on the purchase price, refunds can frequently be more successful than many other promotions at getting moderately loyal consumers of other products to try a competing brand. This may be particularly true when refunds are flagged on the package at the point of purchase, attracting attention at the moment when the consumer is about to buy another brand. (On the other hand, competitive users are much less likely to save a refund offer from mass media and then remember to buy the product, unless their loyalty to their current brand is already weak.)

It is worth noting that the large refund offers needed to attract competitive loyals are likely to be even more attractive to consumers who have sometimes or always purchased the product in the past, and who might well have purchased it now without the refund offer.

This means that large refunds can often result in immediate, substantial financial losses. Thus these refunds are offered mostly on new or low-share brands where competitive users make up most of the population.

Switchers

Refunds may often be successful at getting consumers to purchase one brand rather than another for reasons related to value or variety. They may be an effective tool when the product being sold is of relatively high value and when a sale will be profitable even after the refund has been given to the consumer. In this case the goal is simply to create short-term sales rather than to prompt an increase in long-term value; the fact that the switcher is unlikely to buy the brand on a consistent basis in the future is therefore less crucial.

Refunds that amount to a large percentage of the manufacturer's wholesale price of the product should not be used to generate sales from switchers, however. Obviously, consumers who have purchased the product in the past but continue to buy other brands are unlikely to become much more brand loyal because of one more trial or even a few more trials, even though they may be very likely to take advantage of an attractive refund offer.

Although they may give the sales force "something to talk about" with the trade, refunds are probably less successful than other sales promotion tactics at obtaining and maintaining retail distribution. Refund offers distributed through mass media have very low response rates, meaning that few customers will enter the store looking for the product.

Price Buyers

Price buyers are probably the most likely to take advantage of a big rebate offer; however, they are unlikely to continue to buy the product in the future and will instead purchase whatever competitive item is least expensive. Therefore marketers planning refund programs with high values should find out how many price buyers there are in the category. Running high-value refund offers in categories where a large percentage of consumers are price buyers is likely to be more expensive and less successful at increasing purchases over the long term than is making similar offers in categories that are less price sensitive.

Nonusers

Occasionally nonusers of a particular category may be persuaded to try a particular product if a rebate is large enough; they then may decide they like the product and purchase it again in the future. However, because nonusers of products usually do not even notice promotional materials for those products and generally have reasons for not using a particular kind of product, they are unlikely to take advantage of refund offers.

Refunds and Residual Market Value

When used appropriately, refund offers can have a considerable effect on the value of the brand. A high-value rebate offer can persuade new customers to try the product; if they like it, they may very well buy it again. However, this kind of brand-building activity is likely to come at the expense of current profits, and it therefore is most appropriately used by products that are trying to build market share, such as new products or ones that are currently used by a relatively small percentage of the population. The residual value of this sort of rebate tends to be greatest when the product being promoted has a demonstrable benefit over others in the category, and when it is likely to be used often in the future.

A second way that refunds may in some cases create value is when a promotion that requires multiple purchases of a brand helps to get consumers used to buying a particular product; it may then be more likely that they will continue to buy it in the future. However, consumers who are willing to make multiple purchases in order to obtain a refund are probably more promotion sensitive than the rest of the population; it is therefore fairly likely that they may be tempted by other companies' promotions in the future.

Chapter Eight

Sweepstakes and Contests

Sweepstakes and contests are generally used by marketers as attention getters or excitement builders. Although these kinds of promotions have been used somewhat less broadly in recent years, they are still very effective at addressing certain kinds of marketing problems for specific types of products.

Although consumers may lump contests and sweepstakes into one category, the law makes strong distinctions between the two. Winners in sweepstakes are determined solely by chance, whereas contests require entrants to demonstrate some sort of skill (such as writing a poem or answering a series of questions). Understanding these differences is important because, while consumers entering a contest may be required to purchase the product, sweepstakes must be open to nonbuyers as well as buyers.

Sweepstakes or Contest?

Sweepstakes generally attract more than ten times as many entrants as contests; as a result, sweepstakes are much more widely used by marketers.

About 68 percent of consumers admit to having entered a sweepstakes in the past; far fewer have entered contests. Sweepstakes tend to be more popular with consumers because they are easier to

Exhibit 8.1. Consumers Entering Sweepstakes

Consumers who have entered name in sweepstakes promotion			
	All respondents	Coupon users	Non-users
Yes	68%	70%	62%
No	32%	30%	38%

Source: Courtesy of Manufacturers Coupon Control Center, Clinton, Iowa.

Exhibit 8.2.   Reasons Why Never Entered Sweepstakes*

Reluctance to give name and address	39%
No chance to win	37%
Too much trouble/time/bother	23%
Lack of interest	22%

*Base = Those respondents who have never entered a sweepstakes promotion
Multiple responses allowed

enter; in addition, because sweepstakes target a broader base of consumers, they usually can offer larger prizes.

Because contests have less appeal, they are usually used for much more specialized situations. For instance, Vienna Beef once used a contest that asked consumers to create an advertising slogan for the company's sausage products; the winning slogan was then used in the ad campaign for the product. (It is perhaps worth noting that a professional copywriter won the contest, further demonstrating the difficulty that consumers may have in completing the exercises required in contests.) Contests may also be successful when used to target a specialized group of consumers that might actually be interested in the competition. For instance, sailboat enthusiasts might enjoy participating in a sailing contest, and *Star Trek* fans might be willing to show off their knowledge of the show by participating in a trivia contest.

Sales Force Contests

The most successful contests are often conducted not at the consumer level, but instead are designed to encourage company, distributor, or retail sales forces to work harder to sell the product. For instance, a manufacturer of expensive luggage may reward its top salesperson at the retail level with a new automobile. Or, a company selling computers might reward its entire sales force with a trip to Hawaii if they sell a predetermined number of machines during a certain period in time.

Another related form of promotion is the use of spiffs, which reward retail- or distributor-level salespeople with a certain amount of cash for each item they sell. Retail spiffs are usually offered on relatively high-value products, such as appliances; distributor-level spiffs may be offered either on individual products or on cases of inexpensive products. Although retailer spiffs can be quite successful in getting salespeople to work to persuade consumers to buy a particular brand, they may be frowned upon by some retailers who believe that they reduce sales force credibility among the store's customers, who may rely on salespeople to make unbiased product recommendations.

Another contest used to motivate salespeople at the retail level is the "mystery shopper" approach, a promotion that is announced to retailers in advance. Mystery shoppers usually consist of actors, hired by manufacturers, who visit retail outlets asking for assistance and recommendations. If salespeople respond by suggesting the "right" brand, they can win a prize. The purpose here is to generate awareness and support of the brand at the retail level; these kinds of programs are especially popular in industries where consumers rely on the sales force for assistance, such as the wine or the computer software business.

Although contests can be very useful in motivating sales forces to achieve higher results, the rest of this chapter will focus on the area of consumer contests and sweepstakes. Other trade promotions are covered in Chapter Twelve.

Types of Sweepstakes and Contests

A contest is generally defined as an event that invites the consumer to apply skill to solve or complete a specified problem, such as finish a sentence on why they like the product, add a final line to a jingle, write a limerick, or name a product or trade character. The structure is limited only by the marketer's imagination and goals.

In a contest, entrants may be required to provide a proof of purchase or other consideration to enter, or they may have to satisfy some prerequisite in order to have their entries judged.

Winners of sweepstakes, on the other hand, are determined on the basis of chance. No skill or knowledge is necessary. Although a sponsor may suggest a proof of purchase or other form of entry eligibility, it cannot be required, since doing so would transform the sweepstakes into a lottery, which for-profit organizations may not conduct in the United States.

Sweepstakes may be divided into several different types. In the simplest type, consumers submit their entry forms, and the winner is chosen from all those submitted. Another type assigns numbers to consumers and selects the winner in advance; usually, however, entrants must submit their numbers back to the company in order to be eligible. Finally, sweepstakes may be of the "instant win" type where consumers obtain game pieces and scratch off, peel off, or otherwise remove a covering on the ticket to find out if they have won a prize.

Uses of Sweepstakes and Contests

Probably the most commonly used argument in favor of the use of sweepstakes and contests is that they create excitement and consumer involvement, providing a "shot in the arm" to stimulate sales, usually at a relatively low cost per unit. Well-designed sweepstakes and contests may also extend, build, or reinforce the image or creative positioning of the product by associating it with an appropriate

Exhibit 8.3. Contest: Jim Beam
Source: Courtesy of James B. Beam Distilling Co.

prize structure. Because sweepstakes and contests generate attention, they may also accomplish the difficult task of getting media or direct-marketing advertising noticed and read. Sweepstakes and contests can also be developed and presented to appeal to specific demographic or psychographic segments of the population.

During the past several years, however, sweepstakes and contests have been used much less frequently and for much more specific kinds of programs than in the past. Some marketers believe that consumers have been hit with too many contests, sweepstakes, and lotteries and are therefore becoming less likely to respond to them. In addition, contests and sweepstakes may require heavy advertising support to make them successful, and they may attract many "professional entrants" who have no real interest in the product category. Contests and sweepstakes are also subject to numerous potentially annoying rules and regulations at the federal, state, and local levels, and they cannot be accurately pretested. Most important, however, is probably marketers' impatience with the fact that most sweepstakes and contests seem to be best at creating awareness rather than immediate sales.

Sweepstakes and contests held today are therefore often designed to accomplish particular goals for specific kinds of products. For instance, many sweepstakes are designed to bring consumers closer to purchasing the product through the act of entering the event. When McDonald's runs its "instant win" sweepstakes (such as its successful Monopoly promotion), consumers must stop by one of the restaurants to pick up a game piece. The hope here is that, once in a restaurant, consumers will decide to buy something—and, in fact, these kinds of promotions have been successful both in improving store traffic and in increasing sales. Similarly, in magazine sales sweepstakes, consumers must mail in their order forms to Publishers Clearing House or American Family Publishers to be eligible for sweepstakes prizes; since they are mailing in the entry form anyway, it is likely that many will go ahead and order a magazine.

One of the newer twists in sweepstakes is in making them extremely difficult to enter if no purchase is made. For instance, Publishers Clearing House requires entrants to hunt through materials to find entry stickers making them eligible to win different prizes; purchasing a magazine, on the other hand, enters the consumer in all the contests automatically. This type of design, while annoying some nonconsumers, has been successful in increasing orders, and it has thus far been ruled legal in most situations.

Some organizations also threaten to remove consumers from mailing lists for future contests if they do not buy product when they enter sweepstakes. Although theoretically consumers can write to the company and request an entry form, most realize they are not going to do that and may therefore be slightly more likely to order a magazine in order to stay on the list.

Prizes

The prizes and prize structures of contests and sweepstakes obviously have much to do with ensuring their success or failure. The usual prize structure is a pyramid consisting of a major grand prize of large value, a series of smaller prizes of intermediate value, and a large number of prizes of small or token value (such as samples of the product). However, many companies have recently noted that consumers look more at the value of the prize than at their chance of winning, and therefore they may sacrifice secondary prizes in order to have a very attractive grand prize.

To make a sweepstakes or contest successful, it is important to choose a prize that appeals to the target audience. Cash tends to have the broadest appeal, and it is the most appropriate prize for targeting a mass audience. (Large cash prizes also have the advantage of

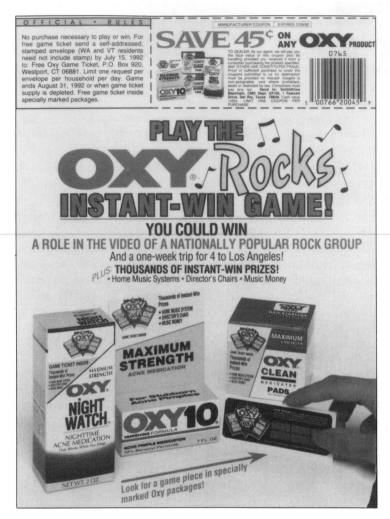

Exhibit 8.4.   A Prize That Can't Be Bought
Source: Courtesy of Smith-Kline Beecham.

allowing companies the opportunity to spread out payment over a large number of years; few companies announce loudly that the $10 million or whatever they're giving away may be worth much less if calculated at the present value of money.)

Although cash is the most frequently used and the most appealing prize, in some cases other prizes, or a selection of prizes, may have even more appeal, particularly if those prizes are difficult to purchase in the marketplace. For instance, teenagers may be excited about the opportunity to meet a movie star, and readers of *Gourmet* magazine may be attracted to the opportunity to attend classes at a top cooking school in Paris. Also, forcing consumers to select prizes they want may cause them to think more seriously about the possibility that they might win something, thereby increasing the likelihood that they will remember to enter.

Costs

Developing and conducting a sweepstakes or contest involves a number of costs:

- Cost of the prizes.
- Cost of the media used to promote the event.
- Cost of entry blanks, point-of-purchase materials, and support activities at both the consumer and trade levels.
- Cost of judging entries and notifying winners. (Several organizations do this on a fee basis. The more requirements in the promotion, the greater the judging fee.)
- Incidental costs, such as legal fees and insurance.

Legal Restrictions

Legal restrictions on sweepstakes and contests are complex, and they may include many state and local regulations. Qualified legal counsel should always be used in developing a contest or sweepstakes to prevent problems from arising. The use of a professional contest developer may also be helpful in simplifying the many details and problems associated with creating a successful contest.

One of the major factors in ensuring the success of this kind of promotion is in having easy-to-understand rules. These will probably include most of the following:

- Clear descriptions of how prizes will be awarded.

- Qualification of entrants. The sponsor of a sweepstakes or contest may limit the requirements for participation, as long as all within a classification are eligible. (For instance, an automobile company can confine its promotion to all licensed drivers; a cigarette company might want to confine its promotions to entrants over 21 years of age. To remove any suspicion of favoritism on the part of sponsors, members of the sponsoring company and its advertising or promotion agencies are almost invariably barred from eligibility.)

- Detailed description of entry requirements (for instance: "Mail entry with bottom panel from carton of Product A or with 3" × 5" sheet of paper on which you have printed the words 'Product A' in plain block letters").

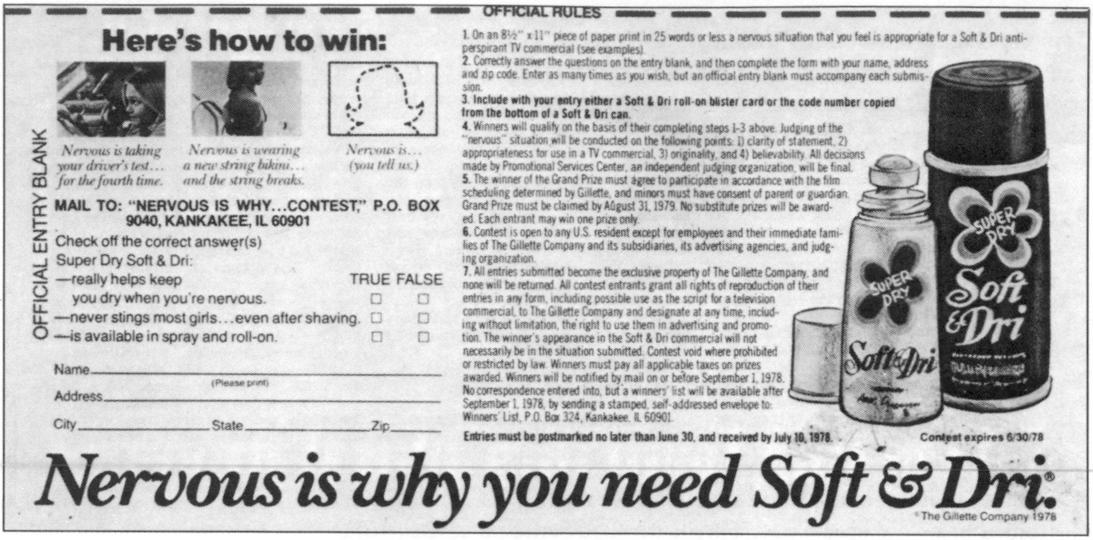

Exhibit 8.5.   Contest Rules
Source: William A. Robinson, *100 Best Sales Promotions* (Chicago: Crain Books, 1980), p. 96.

- Frequency of entry (for instance: "Only one entry per person" or "Enter as often as you like").

- Information on entry cutoff dates, date of drawing, and winners' notification dates. (Two to three months is the usual length of most contests or sweepstakes; this period gives sufficient time for proper marketing promotion and gives more entrants a chance to participate.)

- Legal protection statement. To protect the sponsor from legal complications, the rules usually state "Void where prohibited by law." In cases of sweepstakes, "No purchase required" must be included in the rules.

- Listing of prizes to be given away. In sweepstakes where prize numbers are selected in advance and must be resubmitted to be eligible, it is also important to state what will happen to prizes if winning numbers are not submitted.

- The name of the judging organization and the fact that its decision is final.

- Statement that all entries become the property of the sponsoring organization.

- Statement of situations under which the event may be canceled by the manufacturer. (This has become an especially significant issue following a problem that Kraft had with an instant-win contest,

Exhibit 8.6.   Trip Awarded in an Instant-Win Contest
Source: Courtesy of Continental Baking Company.

where due to a printer's mistake hundreds of purchasers "won" a van that had been intended as a single grand prize.)

Strategic Uses of Sweepstakes and Contests

Because sweepstakes and contests can attract attention and create excitement about a brand, they may sometimes succeed in creating long-term value. Like most promotions, however, sweepstakes and contests work better with certain kinds of consumers and in achieving certain kinds of goals.

Loyal Users

Because sweepstakes may increase excitement and may sometimes convey a product message or benefit, they may be of moderate help in reinforcing sales from current customers.

Certain types of sweepstakes may be successful at obtaining extra sales from current customers. For instance, the aforementioned McDonald's sweepstakes have achieved the goal of getting occasional McDonald's customers to visit the restaurants more often in order to pick up game pieces. However, this is likely to result only in situations where entry in the sweepstakes is very closely connected to purchase behavior.

Some sweepstakes and contests tie together two different products, perhaps in order to give a lift to the less popular one. Although this linkage can result in increased consumer awareness of the secondary product, it is debatable whether any additional sales usually result.

Competitive Loyals

Although competitive loyals may enter a sweepstakes for a product they do not currently buy, they will less frequently purchase the product connected with it. It is only for competitive loyals who buy solely out of inertia that contests may have any effect, as a sweepstakes may occasionally cause an otherwise uninterested person to notice a particular brand. For instance, in some direct-mail sweepstakes, consumers must read promotional materials to enter; if the materials are persuasive, they may consider buying.

Competitive loyals entering a contest may be forced to buy the product; infrequently, this may prompt them to purchase it again in the future.

Switchers

Again, sweepstakes are likely to be successful in getting switchers to consider buying a brand only if entry removes some of the obstacles that usually would cause these consumers to purchase another brand. For instance, a consumer who has to stop at an out-of-the-way grocery store to pick up a contest entry form may also buy some groceries there, rather than making an additional stop at another store.

Consumers who switch brands for reasons of value or variety may sometimes be influenced by sweepstakes promotions because, like advertising, they may offer a reminder to buy a specific brand.

Although contests may cause switchers to purchase a certain product, those consumers are unlikely to continue to do so more frequently in the future.

Price Buyers

For consumers who buy solely on the basis of price, sweepstakes may be ineffective. Most consumers understand that no purchase can be required to enter a sweepstakes, and so they are likely to continue buying their current brand even though they participate in the sweepstakes.

As is the case with other types of consumers, price buyers may occasionally buy a product in order to enter a contest, if the prize is very attractive; however, they should not be expected to do so again in the future unless the brand has strong demonstrable value.

Nonusers

Occasionally, a sweepstakes or contest may bring a product to the attention of nonusers in the category, and they may end up buying the product. For instance, a woman who currently subscribes to no magazines may obtain a Publishers Clearing House mailing and, while glancing through the sweepstakes materials, see a description of a magazine she might like and order it. However, this happens relatively infrequently; what may more often happen is that consumers will enter the sweepstakes without buying any product.

Contests may force nonusers to buy a product at least once, although they are less likely to continue to do so in the future.

Sweepstakes and Contests and Residual Value

Sweepstakes and contests may generate some long-term value in that they may attract attention to brands and may sometimes increase positive feelings among consumers. In addition, a well-chosen prize may sometimes improve the image of the company (for instance, a sweepstakes with a top prize of tickets to Wimbeldon offered by a tennis magazine might reinforce the publication's positioning as an expert in the field of tennis).

Sweepstakes and contests may sometimes increase consumers' propensity to buy a product in the future. As they tend to increase awareness rather than stimulate trial or purchase, they have more in common with advertising and public relations than with other sales promotion tactics. They are therefore often reserved for specific situations where they can be used to encourage immediate purchases, such as in the cases of mail-order or retail companies.

Because purchase can be a requirement for entering them, contests can be more effective at generating trial than sweepstakes and may sometimes influence long-term propensity to buy. However, as mentioned, contests have limited consumer appeal and usually have very low response rates.

Chapter Nine

Through-the-Mail Premiums

Through-the-mail premiums are often good ways to create attention for and excitement about a particular product. Premiums can also be effective at reinforcing brand image and product usage habits, and they may in some cases succeed in getting consumers to buy more of the product than they otherwise might have.

The use of premiums has increased in recent years, although their use is nowhere near that of coupons. Marketers spent $27 billion on premiums in 1989, a 7.1 percent increase over 1988.

Through-the-mail premiums are traditionally divided into two types. Free-in-the-mail premiums are items that are offered free to consumers in exchange for a certain number of proofs of purchase and, perhaps, a small handling charge. Self-liquidators are items that are offered to consumers at a cost; the money received covers the manufacturer's cost of product, making it an inexpensive promotion for the company.

However, an increasing number of through-the-mail premiums combine both of these techniques through what are often called "speed plans," which offer merchandise to consumers in exchange for a few proofs of purchase plus a certain amount of money. This kind of combination allows more attractive merchandise to be offered without forcing consumers to wait a long time to collect many proofs of purchase before they can acquire the premium.

Premium offers today account for a fairly small percentage of consumer sales promotion activities. The reason for this is that relatively few consumers take advantage of premium offers—they often draw redemption rates of only 1 percent or less.

Nevertheless, premiums can be useful in some situations, especially when the premium is an attractive one and when it reinforces the brand's message or benefits in some way.

Exhibit 9.1. Del Monte's Country Yumkins
Source: Courtesy of Del Monte Foods.

Uses of Premium Offers

Premium offers can be an effective way to get attention among a specific group of consumers for a brand that might otherwise appear to be at parity with other products in the category. For instance, if a product has low awareness among a certain consumer group, such as teenagers, a special premium targeted specifically at that group may be successful in attracting attention.

Free or self-liquidating premiums may be successful in providing reminders of the product or reinforcement of the brand message, or in helping consumers to find more uses for a particular product. For example, households that own a Keebler "Hollow Tree" cookie jar may be more frequently reminded of that brand and therefore be more likely to buy Keebler products when in the cookie aisle. Pillsbury offers a free booklet of pizza recipes, which encourages consumers to use the company's refrigerated pizza dough more frequently.

Premium offers can also be helpful in rewarding and, in some cases, increasing the immediate consumption by current users of the brand. For instance, an offer of a free T-shirt may be perceived as a generous gift by users of a particular product, and they may sometimes increase their purchases or buy a larger product package in order to obtain the premium.

Premium offers are usually relatively easy to set up and may be fairly inexpensive in comparison to other types of sales promotions. The only cost in self-liquidators is the advertising and other promotion; in fact, if the premium is priced above the manufacturer's cost, the promotion may even provide a profit. Free-in-the-mail premiums are less likely to be profitable, although the increase in consumer interest in the product and consumer slippage (that is, people who buy the product to obtain the premium but then neglect to send away for it) may make them immediately worthwhile.

Finally, premium offers can be effective ways to obtain names of consumers who buy the product, which may be useful for marketers who are considering implementing or extending direct-marketing programs.

The main concern with through-the-mail promotions is that they commonly do not do a very good job of increasing sales. Many consumers either are not interested in the premium or will not be willing to collect proofs of purchase or pay money for it. Through-the-mail premiums may also be risky to marketers, since if the promotion doesn't go as well as planned, the company may be stuck with the leftover merchandise.

Because premiums are difficult to test, most promotion managers rely on historical experience on their own judgment when developing them. However, the following suggestions and guidelines have been developed.

Premium Selection

Some Guidelines

As mentioned earlier, some of the best premiums (1) reinforce the brand name of the product being promoted and (2) help increase the use of the product. For instance, a soft-drink manufacturer might offer T-shirts that sport a popular advertising slogan (such as Pepsi's "You've Got the Right One Baby, Uh-Huh"); a maker of cake mix might supply a decorative cake pan that is particularly attractive to children and that therefore encourages more frequent cake baking.

It is also important that premiums be perceived as desirable and that they appeal to the appropriate consumer target. Unusual items that cannot be purchased anywhere else often are quite successful, as are items that are less expensive through the promotion than they might be in a retail store.

Exhibit 9.2.   Premium Offer: Colgate-Palmolive
Source: Courtesy of Colgate-Palmolive Company.

Although the total value of a premium is usually fairly small (for instance, no more than $10 or $20), some marketers have had very good experiences with self-liquidators that require the consumer to pay hundreds or even thousands of dollars to obtain them. Consumers who are used to buying from catalogs may be the most attracted to this kind of promotion. The offer of brand name merchandise or of an unconditional guarantee of a refund if the product is not what was expected can also be helpful in making consumers willing to invest in such an expensive item.

Delivery

It is generally very important that through-the-mail premiums be delivered promptly, or at least by the date promised on the order form. This is especially critical in the case of self-liquidators, where consumers have paid money to obtain the premium. If consumers (who in some cases may have ordered the premium for a specific usage occasion or to give as a gift) do not receive the item in a timely fashion, they are likely to be annoyed, and any goodwill generated by the promotion may be lost. If an unexpected delay is experienced (if, for example, demand is larger than expected and additional product must be produced), consumers should be informed of this fact with an apologetic note, and they should be allowed to cancel their orders or (if feasible) choose another item instead.

It is also important that premiums reach the consumer in good condition. Merchandise shipped should include a phone number that can be used to contact the company in the event that merchandise arrives broken or with other problems.

Costs

With free-in-the-mail premiums, fairly expensive items can often be offered by marketers since redemption of the premium will probably be low. These costs, however, should be weighed against the limited benefits that these types of promotions bring.

Another issue is how much to charge the consumer for the products or how many proofs of purchase to require. Most manufacturers choose levels that make the promotion attractive and (for self-liquidators) that result in a small profit or in a not too large loss, with the goal being to create consumer goodwill and to reinforce the brand name rather than to make a lot of money. Even programs that are entirely self-liquidating may require consumers to send in at least one or a few proofs of purchase from the product; this may reinforce the idea that the premium is tied to the product and may also help to generate a few immediate sales.

In addition to the cost of the premium, there are other costs associated with this type of promotion technique:

1. Postage to return the premium. Often this is charged to the consumer as a handling fee. If it is not, it is a cost to the advertiser.

2. Packing and handling the premium. This includes the redemption facility to take care of the orders and the material necessary to ship the premium to the consumer.

3. Any promotional material to be used in the store or returned with the premium, such as a "bounce-back" coupon offer.

Experience shows that it is usually best to pay a fulfillment house to handle the orders and shipping of premiums. Unless an organization has the people and equipment necessary to handle fulfillment properly, it can present a great many problems in terms of time and money.

Exhibit 9.3.   Premium Offer: Uncle Ben's Canoe
Source: Courtesy of Uncle Ben's, Inc.

Promotional Methods

Most premium offers do better if they are promoted in advertising materials. Although the offer of a premium may sometimes give consumers a reason to read an ad, thereby increasing attention for the product, it is obviously expensive to use this method of promotion for any but the most appealing promotion.

Other ways to promote a premium offer are through product packaging or at the point of purchase. Since premium offers do not usually result in strong sales gains, however, retailers may be very reluctant to give messages about through-the-mail premiums any space at the point of purchase.

The Offer and the Return Coupon

Unfortunately, one of the major problems with premiums is that sometimes the marketer makes it difficult for the consumer to understand the offer and even more difficult to obtain the premium. Therefore the offer should be made as clearly and as simply as possible. When practical, it is helpful to show an example of the proof of purchase required and to explain how to remove it. It should also be as easy as possible for consumers to meet the requirements set for redemption.

One of the biggest problems can be the coupon order blank. The blank should include all information needed to fill the order,

Exhibit 9.4. Premium Offer: Pillsbury Glasses
Source: Courtesy of The Pillsbury Company.

including enough room for consumers to supply the required information and spaces for the zip code and other pertinent data.

Timing

Most premiums have very few timing considerations—they tend to work well in any season of the year. The only variables are the lead time necessary for the advertising, the availability of the premium to be distributed, and the necessity of planning around a specific event (such as Christmas).

Premium offers can be started quickly at any time, and many manufacturers have standard items that they hold in reserve for varying market conditions. A major advantage of this type of promotion is that it can be stopped at any time. The only requirement is that orders in process be completed.

Response

Although the traditional method of evaluating a self-liquidating premium offer has been the number of orders filled, this is a fairly

Exhibit 9.5.   Friskies Cat Food
Source: Courtesy of Carnation Company.

inappropriate measure of the success or failure of this sales promotion technique. Objectives set for the sales promotion program in the planning stage should be the basis for evaluation, not the number of premiums redeemed. No one should really care how many premiums are moved except the premium supplier.

As a general guide, self-liquidating and free-in-the-mail premiums often don't achieve orders of much over 1 percent of the gross circulation of the advertising media where the offer appears. For example, if the offer is made in magazines with a total combined circulation of 2,000,000 copies, then returns from the premium would be expected to be in the neighborhood of 20,000. Of course, some offers run well ahead of that mark and some well below it, depending on the premium itself, the audience, the price of the product, and the value of the offer.

It is important in any offer to give complete specifications about the premium in all advertising material. Sizes, colors, and other details must be supplied to help consumers visualize what they are ordering.

Although premiums do not usually have a great immediate effect on sales, they may nevertheless be effective in achieving specific goals with certain kinds of consumers, including attracting interest, reinforcing brand message, and encouraging increased usage.

Strategic Uses of Premium Offers

Loyal Users

Consumers who currently use a particular brand are most likely to be attracted to premiums offered in connection with that product. These consumers already have positive feelings about the product or brand, and so they are more likely to want to wear a T-shirt or use a coffee mug with the brand name on it. Also, because these people are buying the product anyway, they are more likely to be willing to collect proofs of purchase to send in.

After the premium is received, it may remind consumers of the product in the future, thereby promoting further brand loyalty. Finally, consumers who feel that they are getting a "reward" for purchasing the product may feel more positive about it in the future. (This dynamic may be different from the one that occurs with other sales promotion tactics such as couponing, where consumers may begin to believe that the discounted price is the "real" price of the product and may believe in the future that it is worth less.)

Premiums may in some cases encourage consumers to load up on the product or to use it more frequently. Occasionally consumers will buy more of an item in order to be eligible for a premium. More often, as stated earlier, the premium itself will encourage consumers to use the product more. For instance, a manufacturer of Chinese grocery items might encourage purchase and use of its soy sauce and water chestnuts by offering consumers a premium of a wok or a simplified Chinese cookbook.

Competitive Loyals

People who use another brand on a regular basis are unlikely to want an item that features the name of a brand they don't use, and so they are likely to be poor targets for many premiums that serve as reminders of a particular brand. They are also unlikely to purchase a product very many times in order to receive a free-in-the-mail premium.

A self-liquidating premium may, infrequently, be very attractive to the user of a competitive product. When this does happen, the consumer may buy the product to get the required proof of purchase, and trial may be achieved. However, whether this trial converts the consumer into a future buyer depends on a number of factors, such as the quality of the product, previous experience (or lack thereof) with the brand, and the strength of the loyalty to the product currently being used.

Switchers

Switchers may often take advantage of self-liquidating or free-in-the-mail premium offers, although they probably are somewhat less likely to do so than are current loyal users. The strategic benefits of using premiums to attract switchers are basically the same as those achieved with loyal users—possible increased purchases in order to obtain the product, reinforced brand message or increased usage, and goodwill toward the company providing the premium.

Price Buyers

Price buyers may in many cases be attracted to premium offers (especially those that offer merchandise free in the mail or that give a good deal on something they wanted to acquire anyway). However, it is rare that this type of promotion will cause this consumer type to purchase the product beyond what is necessary to obtain the required proofs of purchase to get the premium.

Nonusers

Like competitive loyals, nonusers of a product category are fairly unlikely to be interested in most premiums offered by brands in the category, and they probably will infrequently notice promotional materials for those premiums. Only in the case of a self-liquidating premium (advertised through mass media) that is particularly attractive and a very good deal might they be willing to participate. Although this unlikely scenario may cause these consumers to purchase and try the product, they usually will not continue to do so in the future, unless the product has "hidden" benefits or is markedly better than the others in the category that the nonuser might have tried in the past.

Perhaps the primary reason for manufacturers to offer through-the-mail premiums is the residual value that these types of promotions generate. Although most premiums do not generate a large amount of immediate volume, their continued use in the future can often cause consumers to remember the product better and, possibly, to use more of it. Through-the-mail premiums can also be good attention getters and may promote good feelings about the brand among consumers, increasing the likelihood of obtaining future sales.

Through-the-Mail Premiums and Residual Value

Chapter Ten

Sampling Programs

Sampling is the one sure method of putting a product directly into the consumer's hands. With most other sales promotion techniques, the consumer is required to take an extra step to actually get the product or the reward (such as taking a coupon to the store, making a purchase to get a refund, or signing up for a continuity program). Experience shows that sampling works well as a method of inducing trial of a product. It is particularly effective in introducing new brands or products.

In achieving trial or retrial, however, sampling is not as efficient as couponing—that is, it is generally more successful in generating trial but usually not on as cost-efficient a basis. However, the high trial rate and the extremely good conversion generated by sampling, which turns triers into buyers, usually makes sampling worthwhile.

As effective as sampling is, however, it won't work for all products. Sampling is most successful when the brand has a demonstrable point of difference or advantage over competition—that is, trying the product demonstrates that it is better, more effective, or more efficient. Sampling also works very well for products that can't really be described in advertising and that need to be used or demonstrated for the benefit to be realized. Sampling is particularly costly for products that are highly specialized or that appeal only to small, select markets, such as rug hookers or antique collectors, since these people may be hard to reach and sampling may result in a large amount of waste. Products that appeal to narrow groups that cannot be easily reached should be sampled only if they have important benefits that are readily observed through trial.

Sampling seems to work best for new brands when it is preceded by four to six weeks of advertising. The advertising is used to generate interest, which the sample then converts to trial. There is one major caution with sampling, however. In general, marketers should never sample until there is sufficient distribution in retail stores to support the consumer interest built up by the sample. Nothing turns a consumer off more than to receive a product sample, try it, like it, want to buy it, and then not be able to find the brand in the store.

The general objectives of a sampling program are to stimulate trial of a new or improved product, encourage new use for an established brand, or call attention to a new package. Sampling can be used to build or broaden sales of an established brand in fringe or new geographic areas. It can also be used to encourage trial by a new consumer category or through a new distribution outlet, or to introduce customers just entering the category to the product (such as new mothers to Pampers or 13-year-olds to Clearasil).

Like couponing, sampling is distinguished by the distribution methods used to place the samples in the hands of prospects. As a general rule, the more directly the product is put into the hands of consumers, the more costly it is. Sampling distribution techniques are often limited or dictated by the product itself. If the product is bulky, a through-the-mail sampling plan is probably out. If it is perishable, in-packs or on-packs can't be used.

For most products there are nine major methods of sampling:

Methods of Sampling

Direct Mail

In direct-mail sampling, the sample is sent directly to prospects either through the Postal Service or through an alternative form of delivery. The major problems here are the limitation on what can be mailed or shipped and the expense. New postal restrictions have made sampling by mail somewhat more difficult.

In spite of the problems, experience has shown that direct mail is the best method of sampling and is three to four times more effective than couponing. Direct mail can deliver samples to precisely targeted groups of consumers or to almost every household in the United States. Trial often reaches 70 percent to 80 percent of the homes sampled. The technique is very expensive, however, since the Postal Service charges by the ounce for handling the samples.

Door-to-Door

In door-to-door sampling, the product is personally delivered to the home, usually by an independent delivery or sampling service. The person making the delivery either leaves the sample on the doorstep (or hanging on the doorknob) or delivers it to the person answering the door. This is a very effective but again quite expensive method, probably the most expensive of all sampling techniques. It is best

Exhibit 10.1.   Direct Mail Sample: Crispy Wheats 'n Raisins
Source: Reproduced with the permission of General Mills, Inc.

used with fairly bulky or perishable items in urban areas with high population density. In some communities, however, door-to-door sampling has been outlawed. It is also illegal to put the sampled product into any U.S. mailbox.

Central Location/Demonstrator

Another popular method for putting the product into prospects' hands, and one that may stimulate high consumer involvement, is central-location sampling by demonstrators. The product may be

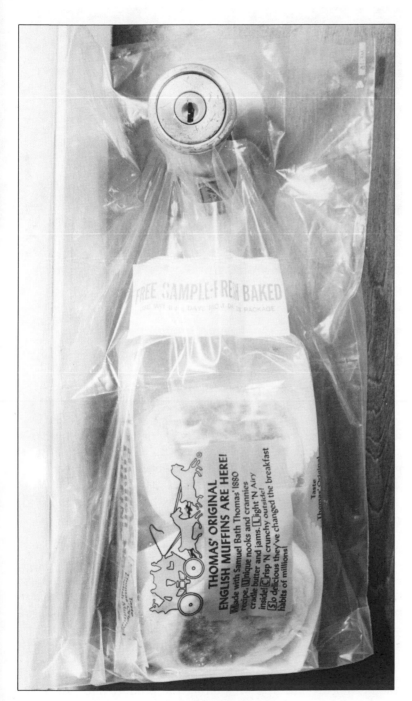

Exhibit 10.2.   Sample: Thomas' English Muffins
Source: Courtesy of Thomas' English Muffins.

Exhibit 10.3.   Sample: Central Location/Demonstration
Source: Courtesy of Stratmar Systems, Inc.

given to prospects in a store, at a shopping mall, on a street corner, at a transportation terminal, or in some other public building. In some cases prospects are given a sample of the product to use later; in other cases consumers may try the product in the setting, perhaps with help from a demonstrator (for example, Pepsi may be compared with Coke, bite-sized pieces of a new sausage may be cooked and distributed on toothpicks, makeup may be applied to the consumer's skin, or a food processor may be demonstrated). This form of sampling is often most effective when accompanied by a coupon or other incentive to purchase while memory of the trial is still fresh.

Co-op or Selective

Market-service groups have organized distribution methods to reach selective population subgroups, such as brides, the military, college students, or new mothers, with a package of noncompeting products that have special appeal to them. For instance, college students may receive a "survival kit" with aspirin, shampoo, and No-Doz upon arriving at school. The major advantage here is the ability to reach targeted groups that might otherwise be difficult to sample efficiently.

Newspapers and Magazines

Few products can be sampled effectively through newspapers and magazines, although there are some exceptions. The best known of these

Exhibit 10.4.   Sample: Co-op Mailing
Source: Courtesy of S. C. Johnson & Son.

are the perfume samples that are often inserted into magazines (and that admittedly annoy some consumers, especially those allergic to perfume). This type of sampling method, of course, can work only for products that are small enough and thin enough to be bound or inserted into the publication. The major advantage of magazines and newspapers is the home delivery of the sample, the ability to reach a selected target, and the opportunity to deliver a sales message at the same time. This sampling method can be expensive, however, because of the necessary production costs. The physical limitations of mass media may prevent samples with any value from being delivered to consumers, with the result that many of the samples may end up going unused.

Sample Packages in Stores

An increasingly important method of sampling is the sale of trial-size packages in the retail store. Miniatures of the product are manufactured and sold to the retailer, who then sells the samples to consumers. This is an effective way to get trial at a very low cost—in fact, there may even be a small profit for the manufacturer and retailer in some situations. Retailers like this sampling method because it gives them margin on samples that might otherwise be given away free.

Another version of this tactic combines several trial-size items in a product line into one item, which is often sold at a premium price. For instance, Kraft encouraged trial of its new non-cheddar Cracker Barrel varieties with a "sampler" that included five 1-ounce flavors of cheese for a relatively low price. The sampler itself appealed to certain kinds of snackers, and it also prompted trial of the new flavors that consumers might have otherwise ignored.

Coupons for Free Samples

Sometimes manufacturers will distribute to consumers coupons that can be exchanged for regular-size containers of the product in a retail outlet. This method of sampling is preferable for products that require extensive testing by consumers before benefits become obvious. In addition, this tactic may be more efficient than others because only consumers who are interested in the product are likely to make the effort to find the product in the store. (A disadvantage, however, is that those consumers who never use coupons will be missed.) Finally, although it can be somewhat more expensive to offer a full-size container of a product to consumers, and although coupons are subject to handling charges (and may be redeemed fraudulently), elimination of the high delivery costs of other methods of sample distribution may make this one worthwhile. It may be especially appropriate for products that are bulky (such as paper towels) or perishable (such as yogurt) and therefore particularly difficult to deliver in any other way.

In-Pack or On-Pack

In some cases a sample may be delivered to consumers with another product from the same manufacturer, serving as a premium. Although this technique is the least expensive way to distribute samples, it also has limited exposure since the sample is distributed

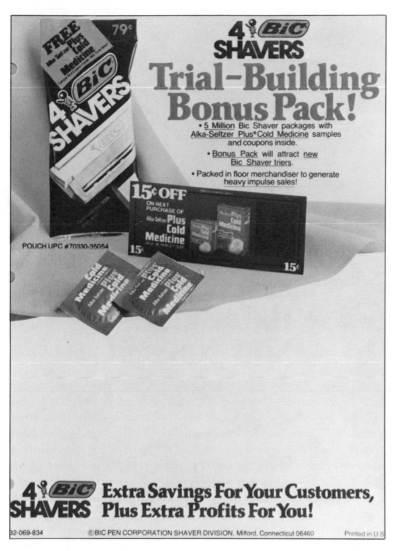

Exhibit 10.5.   Sample: On-Pack Cross-Ruff
Source: A Cross-Ruff Clearing House Promotion.

only to present users of the carrying product. Usually this technique works best with brands that are somehow related to one another, such as coffee and nondairy creamer.

Consumer Request

In some cases, especially when products are expensive or are used by a small percentage of the population, consumers may receive

Exhibit 10.6.   Sample: Dairy Ease Free Sample
Source: Courtesy of Glenbrook Laboratories.

product samples only by request, usually through a mail-in or a toll-free telephone offer. This type of sample may be free or may require a small payment both to defray some of the cost of the product and to demonstrate that consumers are truly serious in their interest. These offers may be publicized through any available means, including mass-media advertising, free-standing inserts, direct mail, in-store displays, in-packs or on-packs, and public relations. For instance, in magazine ads General Foods once offered samples of a new gourmet coffee to consumers calling a toll-free number; Ralston Purina offered samples of its gourmet O.N.E. dog food in free-standing inserts to consumers through direct response. Manufacturers of expensive perfume often offer samples through co-op offers in magazines, with a required payment of $1 or $2 for each sample ordered.

The advantage of this type of self-selected sampling program is that waste is eliminated and, since consumers who respond are likely to be very good prospects, a more attractive sample can be offered. In addition, this type of program can help marketers establish a database of consumers who are likely to be good prospects for the future. For instance, once Ralston Purina obtained a list of dog owners through its sample offer, it would be possible to target them with information on other pet products.

Uses of Samples

As stated earlier, sampling is the most effective way to gain trial for a product, and it is particularly appropriate for products that are new or that suffer from low awareness or small market share. Unlike advertising, which usually takes time to work, sampling may quickly convince consumers to buy a particular product. In fact, in some cases, such as categories with high brand loyalty, sampling may be the *only* way to get consumers to try a new product or brand.

In addition, although the total cost of sampling programs can be high, sampling can be quite efficient at delivering broad-based trial to a majority of the population, or at targeting specific segments. Finally, because sampling is so quick at building demand, the announcement of a major sampling program can be effective in gaining distribution for a new product and, possibly, in getting in-store displays or other trade support.

The main problem with sampling programs is that they tend to be quite expensive and should therefore be considered long-term investments. Products sent through the mail are subject to problems in delivery timeliness and condition, and all methods of distribution may result in theft or pilferage.

Like all promotional programs, of course, sampling works best at building long-term brand value when the product being promoted has some sort of definite advantage over others in the category. This should be considered when predicting the success of a sampling program.

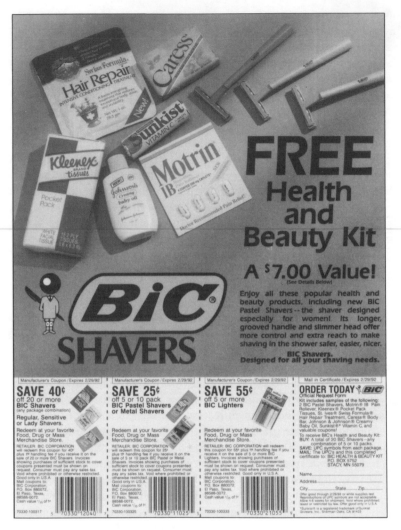

Exhibit 10.7.   Sample: Personal-Care Items
Source: Courtesy of Bic Corporation.

Costs

It is impossible to give accurate costs of sampling programs, simply because they vary so widely and change so rapidly. However, following are illustrations of several methods that can be used by managers to arrive at approximate costs:

1. The cost of direct mail depends on the weight of the product and the postal charges at the time. The cost per ounce to mail a

3-ounce sample in 1991 ranged from 13 cents to 75 cents, based on size and mail class used. In addition to the cost of the sample, other charges that must be included are the mailing list, the carton, the addressing, the handling, the postage, and any return materials (such as coupons).

2. Door-to-door distribution costs vary widely, depending on such variables as the number of homes to be covered, how close together the homes are, the availability of a sampling organization in the community, and the regional location. For example, in Chicago and suburbs the cost of hand-delivering a sample to homes in 1991 was approximately $70 to $95 per thousand. This cost is based on the advertiser furnishing a 3- to 4-ounce sample and the distribution company inserting the sample into a clear plastic bag and hanging the sample on the doorknobs of homes. A coupon can be included for the same cost. It is estimated that each person in the delivery crew can cover about 225 homes per day in fairly compact neighborhoods. (A note of caution: Since some communities have outlawed this kind of sampling, marketers should make sure they are allowed to sample in specific areas before making plans.) Again, the cost of the product, the door-hanger or other method of attaching the product to the doorknobs, and the coupons distributed must be included in the budgeted amount.

3. Usually a flat rate per day is charged for an in-store product demonstrator, regardless of how many units are distributed. In Chicago in 1980, cost per day for a demonstrator was approximately $125 minimum, plus transportation and cost of product. The cost of the product, sales promotion materials, and any coupons that are distributed must also be included.

4. A cooperative mailing to specialized groups is usually less expensive than many other forms of sampling. For example, Donnelley's Carol Wright program has the capability of distributing samples. As with other sampling programs, the cost of the product and any sales promotion materials must be included.

5. The in-pack or on-pack method usually costs less than any other type of sampling. Since the only costs are usually for the product, the attachment or insertion, and any promotional materials, the sample can get to the consumer with little or no actual distribution costs.

As a general rule, the following costs can be incurred in the preparation or execution of a sampling program:

- The sampled product
- Direct-mail or list charges
- Postage or distribution costs

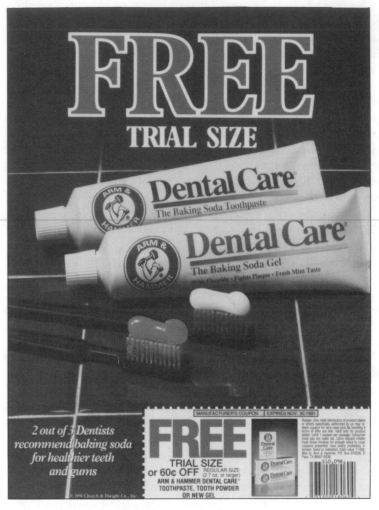

Exhibit 10.8. Sample: Coupon for Free Trial Size
Source: Courtesy of Church & Dwight Co, Inc.

- Handling fees, such as those charged by direct-mail organizations
- Advertising or other sales promotion material costs that might be included in the sample package
- The cost of cartons, boxes, or other materials used to distribute the product
- Retailer and/or clearinghouse charges for coupons distributed with the sample, including the face value of the coupon
- Cost of insertion or attachment for in-pack or on-pack sampling

Exhibit 10.9. Sample: Trial Size Offer through Direct Mail
Source: Courtesy of Ralston Purina Company.

Product Selection

Some products sample better than others. Generally, products that are new or improved and those that have a demonstrable point of difference over competitive brands make the best samples. Often products that are frequently purchased and that have a high number of potential users are especially appropriate for sampling programs.

Products that are less appropriate for sampling programs are those that have slow turnover or those that are not purchased very often. Also, products that require a personal selection or those in which there are a wide variety of choices (such as cologne or cosmetics) usually are successful only when they allow consumers to request the particular items they want or when they can be sampled in-store.

Other products that do not usually do well in sampling programs are those without an obvious consumer benefit or those that are not noticeably different from the competition. As a general rule, mature or established brands do not benefit very much from sampling, unless sampling is done in a new or fringe territory, unless it is targeted at specific kinds of consumers, or unless the product has been reformulated.

Timing

Usually sampling works best if it is done just before any seasonal upswing in sales or use of the product. This helps to generate usage and can result in extra sales.

A general rule of sampling is not to commence the program until there is sufficient retail distribution—normally at least 50 percent distribution in retail stores that would be expected to stock the product. Consumers who try a brand but cannot find it at the retail level may become annoyed and forget about the product.

Size

Although there is no hard-and-fast rule, the sample should always be large enough for consumers to get a fair trial of the product. Of course, that depends on what benefit is being claimed for the product. If it is something that tastes good, one serving can be enough. If it is something that requires continued use to see the benefits, then a larger size to allow multiple use is in order.

As a general rule, a regular size produces more trial than smaller samples, although distributing regular-size samples may also mean that consumers won't have to purchase the products as quickly if they like it. If a smaller size is used, it should be a miniature of the regular package. That way consumers will know what the product looks like when they go to the store to buy it after the trial.

Sampling and Other Forms of Promotion

Generally, sampling should take place following the brand's establishment in retail stores and following its introduction to consumers through advertising. By the time consumers receive their samples (or see offers detailing how to get them), they should ideally already be aware of the product and, perhaps, have an interest in it.

Exhibit 10.10.   Sample: Allerest
Source: Courtesy of Fisons Corporation.

Advertising may also be used to announce that samples are available or that they are currently being distributed, in the case of a broad-based effort. Nutra-Sweet, the manufacturer of the artificial sweetener Equal, even reminded consumers of its sampling of the product with gumballs years *after* the promotional effort, in order to reinforce positive feelings about the product and to increase brand loyalty.

Probably the most effective way to maximize the effect that sampling has on sales is to include a coupon with the sample. For consumers who like the product and who use coupons, this may provide an extra impetus to get them to make that first purchase and to obtain more experience with the product. Of course, this is really appropriate only for products that will be frequently purchased, not for items (such as perfume) that will likely be purchased only occasionally.

Strategic Uses of Sampling Programs

Sampling programs tend to be effective in different kinds of situations compared to other kinds of sales promotion programs. Although sampling may be effective at reminding certain occasional users of the existence of a particular product, it can be even more successful in winning over consumers who currently use other products or even those who currently are nonusers of the product category.

Loyal Users

Consumers who currently are loyal to a brand generally will be unaffected by the receipt of a sample. These people have already tried the product and like it; they do not need any further convincing. Sampling to these consumers may result in sharply reduced profits, since samples are expensive and may substitute for purchases that the consumer might have made.

However, cross-ruffing samples to loyal consumers of other products may be effective. As mentioned, in-packs or on-packs are one of the least expensive ways to distribute samples to consumers. They may be particularly effective when the two products are somehow related—for example, dog food may be a good vehicle in which to distribute samples of a new dog biscuit. This kind of sampling program may even sometimes slightly increase demand for the product being purchased, since inclusion of a sample adds value to it.

Competitive Loyals

Sampling may be very effective at winning over consumers who are current users of competitive products—in fact, sampling may be the *only* way to get many of these consumers to try or consider buying a product other than their regular brand.

In order for sampling programs to be effective with these consumers, however, the product must demonstrate some sort of noticeable superiority to the currently used brand. Advertising or promotional materials should point out this product benefit; the inclusion of a coupon with the sample can reinforce propensity to buy if the consumer reaction is positive.

Switchers

Switchers who have occasionally used a brand in the past are unlikely to be affected very much by sampling programs. Since these consumers already have experience with the product and are still not using it on a regular basis, one more experience with it is not likely to make much difference in their future propensity to buy.

There are exceptions to this, however. One might be when consumers have used a product in the past but for some reason have "forgotten" about it. For instance, Kellogg's Corn Flakes could have conceivably distributed samples of the product to complement its campaign "Taste them again for the first time," which was designed to regain former users of the product. (Whether these consumers would be considered switchers or simply competitive users is debatable, however.)

In-store sampling may also prompt infrequent users to purchase a product (usually an impulse item) when they ordinarily would not do so. Here sampling seems to work well as a point-of-purchase reminder of the product, but it is, of course, even more effective than regular point-of-purchase materials because of the ability of the consumer to actually experience the product.

In certain select cases sampling may also cause switchers or competitive loyals to reevaluate their allegiance (or lack thereof) to a particular brand. For example, the famous "Pepsi Challenge" was designed to convince Coke drinkers or switchers that they really did prefer Pepsi.

As previously mentioned, sampling can be a successful tool in getting distribution for a product, because retailers generally believe that it will increase consumer demand.

Price Buyers

Although price buyers will usually use a free sample, they are generally unlikely to buy it consistently in the future. Only if the quality of the product is so superior to others in the marketplace that it seems to outweigh price considerations in these price-sensitive consumers will they purchase it instead of their regular, inexpensive brand. Since in most categories the differences between products are small, however, this doesn't happen very often.

Nonusers

Sampling is probably the best—and, in many cases, the only—tool that can convince nonusers of a particular product category to begin to use a particular product. Because samples are usually free, their use carries little risk. And once consumers try a product, there is a chance that they will like it and purchase it in the future.

However, although this outcome may occur with some consumers, it is important not to expect a large growth in business from consumers who are not using any product in a particular category. Most nonusers usually have solid reasons for not buying a particular type of product—either they have no need for it or are simply not interested. Usually, only a product that is markedly superior to others on the market, or one that establishes a new category of its own, is likely to convince many nonusers to become future buyers.

Sampling and Residual Market Value

Of all sales promotion techniques, sampling has the potential for the most residual market value. The purpose of sampling is to get consumers to try a product, making it more likely that they will purchase it in the future. The trade-off, however, is that sampling programs tend to be quite expensive and generally do not provide any profits over the short term. They therefore should generally be viewed as brand-building activities designed to increase profits in the future.

Chapter Eleven

Price-Offs

Price-offs flag products on the store shelf so that consumers will notice that they are receiving an immediate discount on the price. For example, a flag, banner, or burst on the package label may read "Save 50 cents" or "Price of product is 75 cents off."

As a promotional device, price-offs fall somewhere between consumer promotions (such as coupons) and trade discounts. Like coupons, price-offs appeal directly to consumers to create attention and demand for the brand. However, like trade discounts, they are used in-store, and they require the cooperation and support of retailers in order to be successful.

While price-offs have certain advantages for the manufacturer, whether they are successful often depends on the type of product being promoted, the competitive situation, and the attitude of the retailer toward the promotion. They therefore are used much less frequently than either coupons or trade discounts.

Uses of Price-Offs

The most obvious benefit of price-offs is that they provide a differentiating factor to consumers at the point of purchase. Consumers who are price sensitive may notice the flagged package on the store shelf and decide to buy the promoted product rather than a competing brand because of the price discount. Therefore price-offs may be more effective in influencing consumers than simply lowering the price of the product, since the flag on the package may catch the attention of consumers who otherwise might not have bothered to compare the prices of all the products in the category.

In addition, price-offs are very flexible for the manufacturer, who can easily control the number of promoted products released into the marketplace. Since the marketer has control over the number of units that are distributed and the geographic area in which the offer will be made, price-offs can be helpful "fire-fighting" tools to

Exhibit 11.1. Price-Off: On the Label
Source: Reproduced with the permission of Hunt-Wesson Foods, Inc.

counter competitive threats in certain marketplaces and at certain times. They also can be used to boost sales of a particular package size, flavor, or brand in a line. For example, if the small size of a product needs a boost, a price-off can be added only to that size to encourage purchases.

Another attractive feature of price-offs to some manufacturers is that, because the company has control over the number of products being distributed, the cost of the promotion can be predicted upfront. This differs from other consumer promotions such as coupons or rebates, where it may be difficult to predict the redemption rate.

However, price-offs also have a number of disadvantages, which explains why they are used less frequently than many other types of promotions. For example, consumers may not always believe that the marked price is "really" discounted, particularly if it is still more expensive than that of competitive products. In addition, laws require that the "regular" price referred to in the price-off must actually be the one charged for the product a certain percentage of the time, which can make price-offs difficult to administer. In addition, if price-offs are used too frequently, they may help to downgrade the image of the brand, so that some consumers begin to believe that it is not "worth" the undiscounted price. This may eventually mean that the product will sell only when it is on discount, thereby cutting into long-term profits.

Another major issue is that, unlike coupons, price-offs are automatically given to all consumers who buy a product, whether or not they would have ordinarily purchased it. This factor may occasionally mean that price-offs are superior to coupons, because they may appeal to consumers who don't use coupons. However, unlike coupons, price-offs have no ability to price tier, or to offer varying prices to different consumers based on their price sensitivity. They are therefore often reserved for categories where a majority of consumers are price sensitive, such as paper towels or dishwashing soap. They also are often restricted to relatively low dollar amounts.

Even more importantly, price-offs have been relatively unpopular with the trade. Retailers must handle products with price-off banners separately from regular-priced merchandise (some of which may already be in stock) in the warehouse and on the store shelf, and must make sure that the amount charged for the product actually reflects the price reduction. In addition, unlike trade discounts (which are often passed on to the consumer as an advertised "special"), price-offs do nothing to generate store traffic for the retailer. Therefore price-off promotions are often not accepted by retailers. It is estimated that only about 50 percent to 60 percent of all food and drug retailers will accept a price-off promotion for use in their stores.

Price-offs also provide special handling problems for the manufacturer. Since price-off packs must be a separate manufacturing run (or must include a special sticker announcing the price reduction), production costs of materials and processing often increase. Also, because the promotion must be offered to all competitive retailers within a market area but may not be accepted by all of them, adequate supplies of regular-priced and special merchandise must both be readily available.

Because of these issues, the use of price-offs by manufacturers has been relatively limited. When price-off promotions are conducted, they are often used to overcome situations where the competition has introduced new or reformulated products or has made changes in pricing, packaging, trade or consumer sales promotions, advertising, or other promotional activities.

Exhibit 11.2.   Price-Off: On Flexible Packaging
Source: William A. Robinson, "Five More 'Best Promotions' Share the Facts and Shed Light on Marketing Success," *Advertising Age,* April 3, 1978, p. 52.

Price-offs tend to be most appealing to the type of consumer who uses other types of sales promotions, such as younger, higher-income, better-educated, urban, married couples with children.

A device similar to price-offs is the use of a prominently featured "Manufacturer's Suggested Retail Price" on the box or package. This type of promotion may help to call attention to the fact that one product is priced lower than others in the category, and (unlike price-off flags) it can be used on a consistent basis rather than only a certain percentage of the time. However, since retailers are unlikely to accept a product marked with a suggested price lower than the one they intend to charge, the suggested price is usually on the high side, meaning that it is advantageous only when the price of the product is substantially lower than that of its competitors. The frequent use of such a tool may also, for good or bad, forever identify the product as a price brand in the minds of consumers.

Some Guidelines

Unfortunately, because price-offs vary so greatly in terms of timing, costs, and production, it is not possible to be very specific about how to use them. There are, however, some general guidelines.

Planning

Price-offs require a great deal of coordination and cooperation throughout the entire manufacturing organization. Since the development of the price-off pack is essentially a manufacturing process (that is, special labels must be affixed or special cartons used in the production run), the production department, the shipping and storage people, the sales force, the wholesaler, and the retailer must all be coordinated so that the promotion is carried out smoothly. A price-off is usually not something that can be developed overnight.

The method of display of the price-off offer on the package is critical to its success. While there is always concern with the attractiveness of the label or feature area, the clarity of the offer and its visibility on the shelf outweigh most aesthetic considerations. If the customer can't see the price-off, it simply won't work. A bold burst (a jagged-edge price spot) or flag (a box printed over the regular label) is best, with the amount clearly stated. The offer should not be hidden.

Generally, a direct price-off will produce faster direct-sales action than any other form of offer. The more complicated the price-off, the lower the interest in the promotion by the consumer.

Costs

Two cost factors should be considered when evaluating a price-off promotion. The first is the cost of the price reduction. This is a fairly straightforward calculation. Simply multiply the number of units on which the price-off is to be used by the amount of the reduction. For example, if the price is to be reduced 10 cents per unit on 100,000 units, the total cost of the reduction would be $10,000. An additional cost that is not quite so easy to calculate is that of the special labels and cartons. Since art work, plates, and special printing are involved, this cost will vary for almost every offer, depending on what is to be done. The production people are the ones most qualified to determine these costs.

Pricing

Price-offs must usually be a minimum of 15 percent to 20 percent off the regular retail price to have much effect with the consumer. As we said before, brands with smaller market shares must usually offer larger reductions than the brand leaders to achieve similar sales increases. Price-offs are also usually more effective for a new brand than for an established brand. New brands can also offer a smaller price reduction than established brands to maximize sale. Usually, the larger the price reduction, the faster the sell-through to the consumer. As you might expect, larger reductions attract more new triers at the retail level.

Usually, smaller quantities offered at greater price reductions will provide larger share increases than offers in which the reduction is smaller but the quantity of goods available is larger. In addition, price-off deals of 6 percent to 7 percent usually have little effect on the product's competitive position no matter what the brand's sales are or the amount of merchandise offered. Lesser reductions only attract the brand's regular users.[1]

Some retailers don't like price-off promotions by manufacturers because they may reduce the profit on the product. For example, most retailers calculate their profit based on what they pay for the product. Thus if they buy a product for 50 cents and take a 20 percent margin, the retail price of the product to the consumer, or the shelf price, would be 60 cents. When a manufacturer reduces the price of the product by a set amount through a price-off on the shelf price, the retailer's margin is also reduced, unless some adjustment is made.

The trade profit on any price-off promotion must be protected. That is, the trade must usually be given a margin equal to or greater than the one being passed through to the consumer through the price-off. For example, if the trade normally receives a 20 percent margin on a product that retails at 50 cents (10 cents per unit) and the price-off to the consumer is 10 cents, then the retailer's margin declines to 8 cents per unit on each sale unless an adjustment is made. In this case, it might be necessary to increase the retailer's margin to 25 percent on the price-off packs to make sure the traditional profit is still received

---

[1]Charles Frederick, Jr., "What Ogilvy & Mather Has Learned About Sales Promotion," speech given to the Association of National Advertisers, September 1973.

on each unit sold. Note that if this is done, the extra discount to the trade on the price-off must be included as a cost of the promotion.

Estimating Supplies

While the supply of price-off units may be estimated on several different bases, it is typically figured as a certain number of weeks of estimated product movement. In other words, the number of price-off units to be offered is determined on the basis of previous or estimated week's sales. Let's assume that sales of Product Alpha have been 100 per week. The manufacturer estimates that sales will increase by 20 percent with the promotion. Thus if the promotion is planned to run 5 weeks, 600 units will be produced (100 units per week plus a 20 percent increase, or 120 units per week × 5 weeks). Usually a 4- to 8-week supply of the price-off merchandise is planned for the average promotion. If the promotion is not being offered in all areas, the promotion amount can be determined by using previous sales or shipments to the specific areas involved.

Federal Trade Commission Regulations

The Federal Trade Commission (FTC) regulations covering a price-off sales promotion program are quite specific. Generally, the FTC requires that:

1. Price-offs may be utilized only by brands with an established retail price.

2. No more than 50 percent of the total volume of a brand may be generated through price-offs in any 12-month period.

3. Only three price-off promotions per year are allowed on any one brand size. A 30-day period must also be allowed between each of the price-off offers on the brand.

4. A price-off must be accompanied by display material that gives the following information clearly:

Brand name	Brand X
Regular price	78¢
Cash savings	12¢
New price	66¢

A retailer who uses this technique must indicate the regular price, the price reduction, and the new price.[2]

---

[2]Sales Promotion Committee, American Association of Advertising Agencies, *Sales Promotion Techniques: A Basic Guidebook* (New York: American Association of Advertising Agencies, 1978), 31–32.

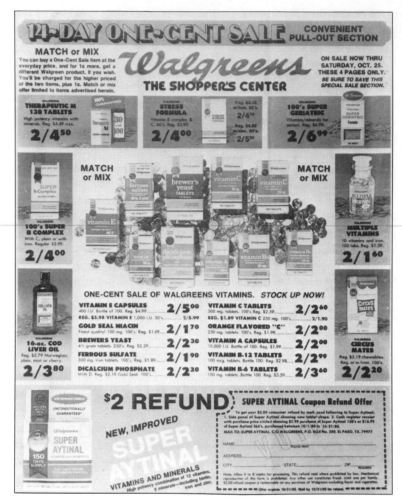

Exhibit 11.4.   Price-Off: One-Cent Sale
Source: Courtesy of Walgreens.

For other legal factors that may affect price-offs for the brand or category, legal counsel should be consulted. Also, the marketer must ascertain that all price-offs are in compliance with current regulations.

Bursts and Flags

When designing a "burst" or a "flag," it is more important to get the price reduction across so shoppers can see it than to have the price look aesthetically pleasing. The only real requirement is that the price reduction not be so large that the general identification of the label is impaired. Shoppers often select products by color and label design, so the label should not be overwhelmed by the "price reduction"—it should be visible at a glance.

Because price-offs attract attention at the point of purchase, they may be successful in winning over certain kinds of consumers who are price sensitive and who are not particularly loyal to a competing product.

Strategic Uses of Price-Offs

Loyal Users

Loyal users are very likely to respond to price-offs, since they offer a "good deal" on a product they like. However, since consumers must be looking in the appropriate section of the store to notice the price-off, it is likely that they would have purchased the product anyway. Although price-offs may sometimes encourage a consumer to purchase more of a product than usual, they usually result in overall reduced profits from loyal users.

Competitive Loyals

Consumers who prefer another company's product are unlikely to be swayed by the relatively low discounts that are usually offered in price-offs. In addition, competitive loyals (even those who usually buy out of inertia) often reach directly for their chosen brand at the point of purchase without even noticing other products or how much they cost. Therefore marketers who hope to lure away competitive loyals are often best off using other promotional tactics.

Switchers

People who use a variety of products in a category are excellent targets for price-off promotions. Consumers who buy a variety of products depending on which one seems to be the best value at the time are likely to notice and be motivated by a price-off promotion. And consumers who switch because they enjoy using a variety of brands may view the price-off as the "tie breaker" that causes them to buy one product rather than another on a particular purchase occasion.

Price-offs are usually perceived negatively by retailers, who may view keeping track of the specially marked product and making sure it is at the right price as a nuisance. Price-offs therefore may result in decreased distribution and increased switching when the product is out of stock.

Price Buyers

Depending on the amount of the discount being offered, price-offs may be very successful in prompting price buyers to purchase a particular product. After the price-off period is over, however, these people will generally go back to whichever brand on the market is the least expensive at the time of purchase.

Nonusers

Consumers who use no products in a particular category are extremely unlikely to be affected by a price-off promotion. In most cases, because these consumers won't even be looking in the section of the store where the product is located, they are very unlikely to notice the promotion or to buy the product.

Price-Offs and Residual Value

Of all sales promotion tactics, price-offs probably do the least for the value of the brand over the long term. Price-offs create little or no consumer trial, meaning that few new sales are likely to be made after the brand goes back to regular price. Price-offs often suggest to consumers that the brand is a value product, which may influence how much they are likely to pay for it in the future. And price-offs are disliked by retailers, meaning that their use can result in decreased distribution. Therefore price-offs probably should be evaluated in the context of short-term profits only.

Chapter Twelve

Trade Deals

Trade allowances, or trade deals, offer some sort of incentive, usually a lower price, to encourage the retailer to do something extra to promote a specific brand. Generally, trade allowances are designed to accomplish one or more of the following four goals: to get retail advertising, retail displays, or retail price promotions, or to either gain or maintain retail distribution.

Trade deals became increasingly popular during the 1980s, and accounted for 44 percent of all packaged-goods marketing expenditures for promotion in 1990. This is largely due to the increasing power of retailers compared to that of manufacturers, a condition caused by declining consumer brand loyalty, product parity, surplus product, and increasing competition among manufacturers for consumer dollars. In order to attract consumer attention at the store level and to maintain the support of retailers, it has become increasingly important for manufacturers to offer various forms of incentives to retailers.

Here are some examples of trade allowances commonly offered by manufacturers:

• *Packaged goods*. Manufacturers offer price reductions to persuade retailers to stock up and to pass savings along to consumers through lower shelf prices. Off-shelf display, advertising, or price reductions may sometimes be required as proof of performance.

• *Cosmetics*. Manufacturers pay for their own demonstrators and sales clerks, and for counter space in department stores. They also may pay "spiffs" as bonuses to retailers' own clerks for selling particular products in a line on a regular basis or during certain time periods.

• *Auto aftermarket*. Manufacturers offer discounts to wholesalers, who may or may not pass them on to retailers.

- *Housewares appliances*. Retailers deduct a "promotional allowance" from the invoice, and manufacturers accept certification that the funds were spent for promotions.

Trade Deals—the Manufacturer's View

Manufacturers may offer trade deals to retailers or wholesalers for two reasons. They may hope to gain short-term volume increases that improve their profits over what ordinarily would have been achieved. They may also hope that the use of trade promotions will increase the viability of the brand over the long term.

Usually, trade promotions are used to increase volume being sold. When a trade discount is offered, the retailer in effect gets a "sale" price and is thus likely to want to buy more of the product. In some cases retailers may stockpile the brand in their warehouses and use it up gradually, thereby eliminating the need to buy as much product later at the regular price. Often, however, retailers may increase their sales volume of the product and move it out of their warehouses immediately by passing some of the discount on to their customers in the form of a "special," causing consumers to buy more of the brand. In addition, retailers may call attention to the lower price by advertising it (for example, in a television or newspaper ad or in a store circular), by setting up a special display for the product in the store, or by calling attention to it at its regular location on the store shelf with a small sign known as a "shelf talker."

Occasionally, manufacturers may benefit from getting retailers to "forward buy" and stockpile merchandise due to a trade discount. For example, a company that has a specific financial or volume goal to meet during a particular quarter or year may choose to load up the trade, even if it means that the organization will sacrifice sales later on. In general, however, for the promotion to be considered a success, it is necessary for at least part of the discount to be passed on to the consumer, thereby increasing retail sales.

For a trade promotion to be judged profitable in the long run, it is necessary that the manufacturer's increase in sales offset the manufacturer's decrease in margin. In addition, it is important to look not only at how much product would ordinarily have been sold during the promotional period, but also at the amount of sales after (and sometimes before) the promotional period that were "cannibalized" by retailers' or consumers' stockpiling the product for use in later periods (or, sometimes, by their allowing inventory to shrink in anticipation of replacing it with product on deal).

For instance, assume that Super Market, a grocery store, would ordinarily purchase 10 units of Brand X each month during January, February, and March at a profit of $10 per unit to the manufacturer;

total profits would therefore be $300. Now, assume that Brand X held a trade promotion during February, reducing the manufacturer's margin to $5 per unit. If Super Market took the opportunity to stockpile the brand while it was on deal, its purchases might be 10 units in January, 20 units in February, and 0 units in March. This would result in a net profit of $200 for Brand X—or $100 less than the company would have earned if no trade deal had been offered.

Now assume that instead of stockpiling the product, Super Market chooses to run an advertised special on it, passing on some of the manufacturer's discount to consumers. If that were to occur, purchases by Super Market might be 10 units in January, 50 units in February, and 10 units in March—for a total of $450 in profits for Brand X. Since this is much higher than the $300 that would have been earned with no promotion, this particular activity would be judged profitable and therefore successful for the manufacturer. The retailer, however, might or might not make a profit on the promotion, depending on the price that was offered to the consumer. Obviously, then, it is important to the manufacturer for the retailer to pass on part of its trade discount to consumers if such a promotion is to be judged profitable for the manufacturer.

Some experts believe that, in addition to short-term profits, trade promotions are capable of providing long-term benefits to manufacturers. For instance, trade promotions can sometimes provide an incentive for retailers to begin or continue to stock a particular brand. In addition, displays or trade advertising may generate attention for a brand, keeping it in the consumer's "evoked set." Trade promotions may also be helpful at warding off competitive threats by preventing another brand from getting retailer support in the immediate future or by loading retailers and consumers with products.

On the other hand, trade promotions can be negative to the perceived value and perhaps the image of brands, especially if they are offered too often.

Trade Deals—the Retailer's View

To understand how to work with retailers on trade promotions, it is important for manufacturers to know what motivates retailers, especially since their behavior in maximizing profit may not always produce the best possible results for the manufacturer.

No matter what type of store is being operated, retailer profits are affected by three major factors: (1) store traffic, or the number of people who come into the store; (2) volume, or how much each shopper, on average, buys from the store; and (3) profit margin, or how much money, on average, the retailer makes on what is sold.

Unlike manufacturers, retailers do not really care which brands consumers purchase while in the store, as long as those products have the same margin. Instead, they are interested in how much money they are making on each customer's "basket" of products and in the total number of customers who visit the store.

Therefore, before retailers will decide to promote a brand (that is, reduce its price, give it display space, and/or advertise it), they are likely to look at the following issues:

1. *Will promoting this item bring business into my store?* Some products, such as coffee or tuna fish, are used by a wide variety of consumers and have relatively high purchase prices. Running promotions on these products may cause many consumers to come to the store specifically to take advantage of the savings that are offered on these products. The retailer's hope is that, once in the store, these people will also purchase other, regular-priced products, thereby boosting total sales and profits for the retailer.

2. *What will running this promotion do to the total sales of the category?* Some products, such as toilet paper, have a finite total demand. Consumers may well take advantage of the low price on a particular brand, but this will usually be at the expense either of sales of other brands in the category (for instance, if the price of Charmin is discounted, the sales of Northern may drop to almost nothing) or of future sales (if consumers stock up, they may not need to buy any more toilet paper for the next month). Deals on other types of products (such as ice cream) may, on the other hand, cause some consumers who wouldn't have ordinarily purchased any product to do so, creating extra total sales for the retailer. In general, retailers are more likely to run promotions that encourage consumers to make additional purchases, rather than to stock up or to switch from one brand to another. (Nevertheless, some retailers do frequently run specials on items like toilet paper, to lure customers into the store, to develop a "low price" image for the store, or to preempt or counter activity from competitive retailers.)

3. *How difficult or expensive would it be for me to store extra product?* A retailer who gets a deal on a bulky product such as paper towels, or on a perishable one such as milk, is likely to find it inefficient or impossible to warehouse the extra product. In that case the retailer will be more likely to promote it, in order to get it off his hands. In other cases where product can be stored inexpensively, stockpiling may be common.

4. *If I promote this item, how much of a discount should I offer?* When determining how much to discount the price of a brand,

retailers take into consideration their current margin on the brand, the discount being given to them by the manufacturer, and the potential for increased brand and category sales. Retailers will sometimes lower the price of a product by more than the discount they are getting from the manufacturer, but they will more commonly pass on only part of the manufacturer discount.

In the retailer's decision to promote or not promote a particular product, the answers to these price, volume, and margin questions are generally much more important than any persuasive actions on the part of the manufacturer. By keeping these issues in mind, manufacturers are more likely to be able to create trade promotions that are likely to have an impact on total sales over time.

Trade Advertising, Displays, and Price Discounts

Sometimes, manufacturers may offer trade deals to retailers simply to obtain or maintain distribution. Usually, however, they hope that the trade deal will increase sales to the consumer by getting the retailer to offer a price discount on the product, to advertise it in the media or in store circulars, or to put it on display.

Price discounts generally have a large effect on the sales of brands to consumers, especially if they are advertised or featured in some way. Retailers can offer price discounts by reducing the amount charged for the brand, by offering an in-store coupon, or by giving extra product (for instance, "two for the price of one").

Trade advertising is generally paired with price discounts, increasing the number of people who become aware of the special and increasing the likelihood that they will visit the store to take advantage of it. Retailers may mention the special on the brand in television or radio commercials, in print advertising, or in store circulars. In some cases print advertising may include a trade coupon, which must be presented to the retailer in order to receive the discount.

Displays in the retail store draw attention to particular brands. Although displays can be successful at moving additional product at the regular price by attracting the attention of hurried shoppers, they are often paired with discounts to encourage maximum sales increases. Displays for brands may be located at the front of the store, at the end of an aisle, or in an aisle; in addition, "shelf talkers" may call attention to the brand at its regular spot on the shelf. Displays are often awarded to large, bulky products, since it might be difficult to store enough on the shelf to satisfy consumer demand for the product at a reduced price.

Types of Trade Discounts

Discounts may be offered to retailers in a number of ways. Some of these discounts force retailers to meet certain requirements, such as providing proof of advertising or displays; others have no such requirements.

In this section, to simplify the discussion, it is assumed that the manufacturer sells directly to the retailer with no wholesaler or distributor involved. However, in many cases trade promotions are developed by the manufacturer and offered to the wholesaler, who may choose either to improve the offers or to not pass some of the discounts on. Rather than explain this complex world of multiple discounts, the steps are simplified here for the sake of clarity. The basic concepts of each type of trade promotion can be then made to fit individual buying categories and the various methods of product distribution.

Buying Allowance

The buying allowance is simply a discount on the purchase of a brand at a certain time. For example, the manufacturer might offer the retailer a buying allowance of $1 per case for all cases purchased during the month of November. However, a buying allowance is often tied to the purchase of a certain number of units. For example, the manufacturer's buying allowance of $1 per case might be allowed on all purchases if 10 or more cases are purchased at one time. Or it might apply to all cases the retailer purchases in excess of the average purchased during the same period the previous year. In most instances the allowance is either deducted from the invoice or given as credit.

Usually, the purpose of a buying allowance is simply to gain or retain retail distribution or to attempt to obtain a lower shelf price to the consumer. Often it is used to ward off competition or to load retailers prior to an anticipated competitive trade deal. While the allowance can be instituted quickly and easily and requires no special handling by the manufacturer, the retailer is not required to promote the offer in any way or to pass the savings along to the consumer. Thus, while the objective of the manufacturer might be to obtain retail price features at the store level, the retailer may absorb the discount or allowance and take it as extra margin on the product.

Although the buying allowance is by far the most popular form of trade allowance, it often results in the least action at the consumer level.

Off-Invoice Allowance

While the buying allowance usually applies to some form of quantity discount, the off-invoice allowance normally refers to a price reduction for a certain period of time. For example, again assume that the manufacturer offers a $1 per case allowance. In this instance, however, the discount is allowed on all purchases made between March 1 and April 15. It makes no difference how many cases the retailer purchases, but the purchases must be made between those dates to earn the discount. In addition, the allowance is deducted directly from the invoice for the products. For example, if the product regularly sold for $10 per case and the retailer purchased 100 cases, the cost would be $1,000. With an off-invoice allowance, however, the manufacturer would submit an invoice for $1,000 less the $100 ($1 per case on 100 cases), making a net invoice to the retailer of $900.

Manufacturers like this sort of trade allowance simply because it is fast and easy, and the retailer understands it and is accustomed to using it. Sometimes manufacturers can convince the retailer to offer a price discount to the consumer because of the off-invoice allowance, since the offer is for a limited period of time.

The basic promotion difficulty with the off-invoice allowance is simply that the retailer may stockpile the product at the reduced price to sell later at a greater margin. There is usually no requirement that the retailer pass the reduced price along to the consumer now or at any later time.

Free Goods

In a free-goods offer, the manufacturer offers an additional "free" amount of the product with the purchase of a minimum quantity. A typical offer might be to give one case free with the purchase of 12—a "baker's dozen." Normally, the free goods offer is for a limited time and may or may not be for a one-time purchase. For example, the offer might be for the period May 1 through July 15, or it might be limited to the next order the retailer places within a certain time.

Manufacturers particularly like the free-goods offer because the only cost is the product being offered. This is actually the lowest net cost discount that the manufacturer can give. Here's why: Assume the cost to manufacture the product is $5 per case, and the normal wholesale price to the retailer is $10 per case. If the offer of one free case with the purchase of 10 were made, the discount cost per case on the product sold would be only 50 cents (10 cases are sold; one free case at a cost of $5 is given in the deal; $5 ÷ 10 cases = 50 cents per case). On the other hand, a buying allowance or off-invoice allowance would normally amount to more—for example, the $1 per case allowance mentioned above. While the free goods offer in our example sounds much more impressive than the offer of 50 cents off per case, it actually amounts to the same net income to the manufacturer.

Some manufacturers also prefer the free-goods allowance because it may encourage the retailer to purchase more during a specific period of time. As a result of a free-goods allowance, the retailer can often be encouraged to pass part of the savings along to the consumer, since he actually receives the selling price of the free goods as profit.

A free-goods allowance is an excellent trade promotion for many types of products. It doesn't work well, however, on slow-moving items. The retailer simply won't stock up on or promote a product that sells only a few units per week.

Dating

Though technically not a form of trade allowance, dating is included because it involves a form of discount or method of dealer allowance. Dating simply means that the retailer can purchase a certain amount of product now and be billed for it over a period of time. In some cases purchases may be made now at a reduced price and shipped at a later date. For example, assume the retailer purchases $750 worth of merchandise from the manufacturer on June 1. With dating, he might pay $250 on August 1, another $250 on September 1, and the final $250 on October 1. In this way, the retailer is not obligated to pay for the merchandise in advance but can spread out the payments as the merchandise is sold in the retail store. In effect, the manufacturer is financing the purchase but at no interest.

Manufacturers like the idea of dating simply because it is a fairly inexpensive form of merchandising to the trade. It can often help them save warehousing costs because they move the product out of their plant and into the warehouse or storage area of the retailer. It is a particularly good way to move seasonal goods. For example, snowblowers may be sold and shipped to the retailer in April, May, and June with datings of October, November, and December. This allows the manufacturer to encourage the retailer to have the product on hand for the selling season, yet it still allows him to maintain a reasonable production schedule. Some manufacturers, particularly those whose products are high volume and fast moving, avoid dating because they are essentially financing the retailer to sell the products. Dating can obviously become a financial problem if done to excess.

Dating is typically done on fairly high-priced, slow-moving items, such as tires, batteries, some larger appliances, and seasonal equipment and materials.

Cash Rebate

This is the simplest form of performance contract. The manufacturer agrees to give the retailer a cash discount of some sort (so much per case, a percentage of the total), provided the retailer does a mutually agreed-upon task. That might be simply to stock the product, increase the shelf space, or purchase and display the full line. When proof of the performance of the task is provided, the manufacturer sends the retailer a check for the amount of the discount. While the agreement may be that the cash rebate will be paid upon performance, sometimes the retailer wants the money in advance. This can create a ticklish problem for the manufacturer, particularly if the retailer is a large account.

The major advantage of a cash rebate to the manufacturer is that the retailer must perform prior to payment. This enables the manufacturer to police the offer with the retailer and make sure the agreement is complied with.

In some cases retailers may receive an annual rebate of a fixed percentage of all purchases made throughout the year or on all purchases over a certain set amount. For instance, retailers may receive a 2 percent discount in January on all of the dollar volume over $100,000 spent throughout the previous year.

Advertising or Display Allowance

Similar to the cash rebate is the advertising or display allowance. Again, the retailer must perform some function or service to earn the discount. The difference here is that normally the discount earned is in the form of a credit memo rather than cash. Additionally, the task to be performed by the retailer usually has to do with some sort of consumer offer, such as a display, a reduced-price special advertised in the newspaper, a price-off shelf feature, or the like. Usually, the advertising allowance requires the placement of space or time media to promote the product. The display requirement, on the other hand, normally involves in-store presentation of the product.

The advertising or display allowance is commonly written into a contract between the manufacturer and the retailer. As part of a contract, the advertising allowance is much easier to enforce, since the allowance need not be paid until after proof of performance is submitted. The proof usually consists of tear sheets of newspaper ads, copies of shelf signs, pictures of displays built, or other verification that the contract was completed.

For example, the manufacturer might give a $1.50 per case advertising allowance on a purchase if the retailer agrees to reduce the price of the product to the consumer and promote that price reduction in the outlet's regular newspaper advertisement. Usually, there are stipulations on how the advertisement must appear; that is, it must be a certain size, must appear within the main section of the newspaper ad, must be a price reduction below normal retail, and so on. The manufacturer cannot specify the amount of the reduction since this would amount to price fixing.

Other types of advertising or display allowances include a case or unit reduction for a feature with a shelf sign or a shelf-price reduction. Displays are usually rewarded on the basis of a flat amount per display or on a sliding scale based on the size of the display. There are literally hundreds of variations on the advertising and display allowance approach, and some are used more widely in certain product categories than in others.

The usual reason for an advertising or display allowance is to encourage some sort of retail activity in the store. It is also widely used to gain or hold retailers in the distribution system or to counter competitive activity.

The advertising or display allowance is easy to set up. Since it is established by contract, most retailers perform as expected. Some retailers try to take advantage of the contract and do only the minimum required. They may, for example, build only a few displays, run only the smallest possible newspaper advertisement, or offer the smallest discount to the consumer. There is little the manufacturer can do about this if the retailer has complied with the actual terms of the contract.

Count-and-Recount Allowance

The count-and-recount allowance is a special type of trade deal designed primarily to get the product from the wholesaler or retailer's warehouse to the stores or to reduce inventory. The reason for this strategy is that retail stores have little space for storage. Therefore, if the product is shipped to the store, it will likely be displayed and sold.

The count-and-recount allowance works this way: The manufacturer agrees to pay a given sum based on the opening inventory in the store or warehouse, plus the amount of product purchased, less the ending inventory in the store or warehouse. This is usually tied to a period of time, such as 60 or 90 days. For example, assume that the product being promoted is canned applesauce. The offer the manufacturer makes is that a credit of $1.50 per case will be given on all cases moved through the store or warehouse during the June 1–July 31 period.

On June 1 a count is taken of the amount of canned applesauce in the store or warehouse. Assume it is 150 cases. During the time of the promotion, the retailer buys and is shipped an additional 200 cases of canned applesauce (for a total of 350 cases). On July 31 another count of the canned applesauce is made in the store or warehouse. This count shows 65 cases are still in inventory. The retailer is thus entitled to a credit of $427.50 as shown below. The $427.50 discount is then sent to the retailer in the form of a credit memo.

Opening inventory	150 cases
Purchases	+ 200 cases
Subtotal	350 cases
Less inventory on hand	− 65 cases
Entitled to credit	285 cases
Allowance per case	× $1.50
Total credit	$427.50

Count-and-recount allowances are primarily used by manufacturers to flush the inventory of a new package or an improved product out of the warehouse into the retail stores or simply to encourage more retail activity on the brand. They can help solve out-of-stock problems at the retail level because they force the product onto the shelf. In addition, count-and-recount allowances can often be used to help force a lower shelf price or feature on the brand at the retail store.

Manufacturers like this sales promotion technique because it is easy to institute. No shipments or sales are required to get it going. In addition, the count-and-recount offer is paid only on the product that is sold or moved.

Unfortunately, the retailer is not forced to act with this sort of sales promotion device. He may only increase his stock of the product at the store level and not increase sales. This type of promotion also requires a large amount of the manufacturer's sales force's time to set it up and carry it through. The biggest disadvantage to the manufacturer is that there is no incentive to restock the warehouse. In the illustration above, the warehouse stock declined from 150 cases to 65 cases. With this type of inventory, the retailer is not likely to develop any sort of promotional activity but may be content just to hold the smaller stock.

Although count-and-recount allowances can be tedious to administer, the concept has the potential of being applied in a new way with the use of scanner technology. Scanner data can be used to inform the manufacturer of how many units of a particular product were sold by retailers during a particular promotion period, and therefore how much of a discount should be given.

Although the use of scanner data and count-recount may ensure that more of the discount of a product is passed on to the consumer, thereby increasing sales in the long run, retailers may find these types of monitoring systems to be annoying. Therefore manufacturers may need to offer a particularly good deal to persuade retailers to participate.

Buy-Back Allowance

In an attempt to solve the problem of restocking the store or warehouse after a count-and-recount allowance, a buy-back allowance may be offered. This simply consists of a "deal" to encourage bringing the store or warehouse stock level up or back to where it was prior to the time the count-and-recount allowance was given. It works this way.

Let's use the canned applesauce example again. At the end of the promotion period, the warehouse has only 65 cases in stock. A buy-back allowance of $1 per case might be made on enough cases to bring the stock level back to its original starting point. (In our example this would be a total of 150 cases.) An alternative is to limit the allowance to the number of cases sold during the count-and-recount allowance. (In the above example this would have been 285 cases: 350 cases on hand or purchased, less 65 cases on hand at the end of the promotion.) If the buy-back were limited to an amount intended to bring the inventory level back to the starting point, the retailer could buy a total of 85 cases (150 starting inventory minus 65 cases ending inventory) at a $1 per case discount. This would amount to a credit of $85. If the limit were the number of cases moved, the retailer could purchase 285 cases. At the discount of $1 each, this would be a total of $285. In most instances the buy-back allowance is on a single purchase at one given time, and the discount generated is given in the form of a credit memo against the purchases made. Usually it is limited to the amount of merchandise purchased during the previous period.

Manufacturers like the buy-back allowance because it is an incentive to the dealer to restock the warehouse. Retailers like it for the same reason, since it allows them to bring their warehouse stock up to the previous level at a reduced price.

Although the retailer is not required to pass any of the savings on a buy-back allowance along to the consumer, the manufacturer does have control over the promotion, and there is usually a set limit on what is offered.

Although proof of performance is listed in each of the above trade promotions, it is very hard to enforce. If the retailer wants to, he can cheat or totally avoid fulfilling the contract. There is little recourse for the manufacturer except to attempt better persuasion tactics in the future.

Spiffs and Mystery Shopper Programs

Spiffs and mystery shopper programs attempt to influence salesperson behavior in categories where recommendations are important. In spiff programs, manufacturers pay members of the retail sales force a set commission on every item sold during a particular time period. "Mystery shoppers" visit stores anonymously and give gifts or cash to salespeople who recommend the "right" brand. (See Chapter 8 for more information on spiffs and mystery shopper programs.)

Slotting Allowances

Although slotting allowances are not considered a usual trade deal, they have become increasingly important elements in retailer decisions on stocking new products.

To begin to stock a new product or a new-product size, retailers incur significant administrative expenses. They must make room for the brand in the warehouse (reserving a "slot" for it), must build it into their inventory systems, must reconfigure store shelves in each unit to include the new item, and must reprogram their wholesale and retail computers. Since U.S. manufacturers introduce nearly 10,000 new products each year (including various sizes and varieties of new and existing products), these expenses can be significant.

The amount of the expense can be particularly annoying to retailers because new brands often do not cause consumers to buy more total product, but rather to shift existing purchases to the new product. (For instance, consumers may purchase a new brand of cookies rather than their old standby brand.) Therefore retailers have attempted to use slotting allowances to pass on some of their administrative costs for new brands to the manufacturer, who will ultimately benefit more from the success of a new brand than the retailer will.

Slotting allowances are the one-time fees that retailers charge for the introduction of a new product, or a new size or flavor, into a new store. Slotting allowances typically run $15–$25 per store; considering that there are approximately 30,000 major grocery stores in the United States, the amount of money in slotting allowances that major manufacturers must pay to roll out a new product nationwide can be considerable. Retailers defend these fees, how-

Exhibit 12.1. Trade Coupons: In-Ad
Source: Courtesy of Walgreens Drug Stores.

ever, by stating that in addition to paying for administrative costs, slotting allowances cause manufacturers to introduce only those new products that they are confident will succeed.

An alternative to slotting allowances are the so-called "failure fees," which are paid by manufacturers only if one of their new or recently introduced products must be removed from store shelves because of poor sales. Failure fees, which are higher than slotting allowances, give manufacturers an extra incentive to introduce only products with high potential and to support them to make certain they succeed.

Although slotting allowances generally apply to most brands, they are sometimes waived by retailers who want to stock a particular item. These special items may include a size needed to round out a store's variety of products, a specialty item not manufactured by other companies, or a product that is certain to have high consumer demand.

Trade Coupons

Trade coupons are distributed by retailers and are good only on specific brands at the store that is offering the coupon. Trade coupons are usually valid only for a week or two, in order to get people into the store during a specific period of time.

Usually, the manufacturer agrees to reimburse the retailer a certain amount per coupon for all coupons redeemed. The manufacturer may reimburse the retailer for the full face value of the coupon or for less, depending on the agreement. In addition, some manufac-

Exhibit 12.2.   Trade Coupon: On the Shelf
Source: Dominick's Fine Foods, operators of 70 high-quality, high-volume supermarkets in the Chicagoland area.

turers may provide limits on the number of coupons that will be reimbursed or on the total amount of payment, in order to be able to more carefully predict expenses and to control the amount of retailer misredemption.

From the manufacturer's point of view, the primary advantage of trade coupons is the assurance that a proposed price reduction will be passed on to the consumer, and that it will be necessary to pay only for actual sales from price-sensitive consumers over a limited period of time. Retailers may see trade coupons as a way to maintain a low-price image, to generate store traffic, or to differentiate themselves from competition.

Trade coupons may be distributed by the retailer in a number of different ways. They may appear in ads, in coupon flyers, or in the store at the door or near the product.

Trade coupons may be especially effective in competitive situations. For example, a trade coupon featured by a major retailer may preclude the use of a competitive feature offered at the same time by other retailers in the market. Trade coupons may also work well at opening new territories or introducing new products, since customers may transfer acceptance from the retailer to the brand. In addition, trade coupons (unlike other trade promotions) are a guaranteed way to get a price reduction or other offer to the consumer.

Many retailers, however, have moved away from requiring that consumers present actual coupons; instead, they just give the dis-

Exhibit 12.3.   Trade Allowance: Free Goods
Source: Courtesy of Duro-Lite Lamps, Inc.

count to everyone purchasing the product. Although eliminating the need for the presentation of coupons can be convenient for retailers and consumers, it can make it more difficult for manufacturers to keep track of how many units were purchased. Scanner data may be helpful as a replacement.

Certain legal and practical considerations place some constraints on the ways that manufacturers can use trade promotions. For instance, manufacturers are not allowed to require that retailers pass on any part of trade allowances to consumers. In addition, manufacturers must offer the same or a proportionately equal discount to all competing retailers within a defined geographic area, meaning that discounts cannot be used to reinforce sales at some retailers in an area but not others (FTC Robinson-Patman regulations). Diverters (agents who buy product at a discount in one area of the country, then move it to other regions where it's not on sale, and resell it) may also make it impractical to offer trade deals that differ substantially on a geographic basis.

Also, even though it is legal for manufacturers to require retailers to run advertising or to display products in order to receive a trade deal, it may be difficult to monitor whether these activities actually were conducted. Even if the manufacturer does determine that a particular retailer didn't comply with a specific requirement for a promotional allowance, it may be difficult to recoup that money without jeopardizing future trade relations.

Limitations of Trade Deals

Trade deals can be effective at creating attention for a brand and at creating a sharp spike in sales over a short period of time. However, trade deals tend to be most effective when they are run for relatively short periods and at relatively infrequent intervals. If deals on a particular brand become too prevalent, both retailers and (if the retailer passes on part of the discount) consumers may begin to see the discounted price as the regular price and therefore become less responsive.

Trade promotions tend to work best when brands being promoted have high holding costs for the retailer, and when promotions on the particular brand cause consumers to purchase more of it. This dynamic is explained in the Blattberg trade promotion grid, developed by Professor Robert Blattberg of Northwestern University (see Exhibit 12.4).

For instance, a bulky product that is promotionally responsive, such as soft drinks, is likely to be very successful when offered with a promotion to the trade. Because consumers are interested in the product, retailers are likely to pass on the discount to the consumer and to advertise the special, producing a sharp increase in sales. In addition, because retailers are unable to store much of the product, future sales will not be cannibalized. The main problem with this type of product is that manufacturers may find promotions so successful that they tend to overuse them, diluting

Uses of Trade Promotions

Retailer Holding Cost

	High	Low

	Great to Promote
	• increased sales
	• little stockpiling
	
	(soft drinks,
	paper towels)
		Huge Sales Spikes
		• increased consumer
		  sales
		
		• high retailer
		  stockpiling
		
		(canned tuna,
		  coffee)

	Few Additional Sales
	from Consumer or
	Retailers
	
	(dry dog food,
	bottled water)
		Awful to Promote
		• few extra
		  consumer sales
		
		• high retailer
		  stockpiling
		
		(laxatives, spices)

Exhibit 12.4. Blattberg Trade Promotion Grid
Source: Developed by Robert C. Blattberg, Northwestern University.

the image of the brand and causing some consumers to purchase only on deal—as apparently has happened in the soft drink and paper towel categories.

In situations where holding costs are high and promotional responsiveness is low, trade promotions are not very likely to increase sales for the manufacturer. For instance, because large sizes of dry dog food are difficult to store and appeal to only a small percentage of the population, they are promoted relatively infrequently.

When promotional responsiveness is high and manufacturer holding costs are low, trade deals may produce extremely high incremental sales, as both consumers and retailers stock up. However, this is likely to be at the expense of some future sales, due to the large amount of product getting stockpiled by the retailer (and possibly by the consumer). For example, a deal on canned tuna fish may be passed on to the consumer, resulting in incremental volume; however, since tuna is compact and easily stored, it is also likely to be stockpiled by retailers and consumers. Promotions on these kinds of products can generally be useful if used relatively infrequently.

Brands that have low retailer holding costs and low consumer responsiveness may result in sales spikes through trade promotions; however, nearly all of the extra volume sold is likely to be "borrowed" from future sales, since retailers will stockpile product and won't have to buy it as quickly in the future. For instance, laxatives and other over-the-counter medications are usually compact and easy for retailers to store for long periods of time; in addition, promotional responsiveness is likely to be limited, since only a finite percentage of consumers use any particular pharmaceutical, and since even those consumers' usage is not likely to increase simply because the brand is on deal. Brands that fall into this category are generally not good candidates for trade promotion, since immediate incremental volume is likely to be at the expense of long-term profits.

One positive feature of trade deals is that they can be implemented quickly; all that is necessary is to work out an agreement with retailers. They can therefore be effective in "fire-fighting" situations, such as when competition has become more aggressive (by, for instance, increasing advertising or introducing a new brand) in a particular market.

Ensuring Retailer Performance

Although policing trade deals and following up on retailer performance are difficult, there are some guidelines manufacturers can follow:

• Tie the trade allowance to a cooperative advertising allowance requirement and demand proof of advertising. By tying the two together, the manufacturer is at least contractually entitled to determine whether or not the contract has been fulfilled.

• Require proof of the price reduction. This can take the form of tear sheets of advertising, shelf markers, or the like. Have the retailer send something to prove that the price was actually reduced as agreed.

• Set up a store-monitoring system. This can be done through part-time help in various markets at a very reasonable cost. It also helps verify that the displays were built according to contract agreement on size, number, and location.

• Handle the verification elements of the trade allowance through the advertising, sales promotion, or product manager, not through the sales force. When you turn the sales force into policemen, you weaken their sales effectiveness.

Strategic Uses of Trade Deals

Trade deals are frequently cited as the most misused and overused form of sales promotion. However, when used appropriately, they can be useful in helping certain kinds of marketers to reach specific goals. (Much of this success, of course, depends on how much of the trade promotion is passed on to the consumer in the form of price reductions, advertising, trade coupons or displays. This section examines how consumers are likely to respond to deals when they are passed on by the retailer who receives them from manufacturers.)

Loyal Users

Trade promotions may encourage some current customers to remain loyal to a particular product rather than switching to a competitive brand. They may therefore be very effective when used as a countering move when competitors have begun (or are expected to begin) making active attempts to steal a brand's loyal customers (for instance, with heavy advertising, a new or reformulated product or a sampling program). However, often brand loyal consumers who buy a product that is on a retailer "special" would have purchased it anyway, either immediately or in the future.

Trade deals that are passed on to consumers may be very successful in getting loyal users to make additional purchases when the extra product may be easily consumed. For instance, an occasional user of the relatively high-priced General Foods International Coffees brand may purchase a can to have as a special treat if it is on discount.

Competitive Loyals

Trade deals are usually less successful than other promotions at getting competitive loyals to buy a particular brand, even when the discount is passed on to the consumer. Consumers who are consistently loyal to another brand probably won't be motivated to switch when presented with a simple price decrease, and possibly they won't even notice the promotion. However, trade deals, like other forms of sales promotion, may help to convert competitive loyals when combined with other forms of promotion that catch these consumers' attention, such as advertising, public relations, or sweepstakes.

Switchers

People who switch for reasons of price or variety are often good targets for trade promotions. The increase in the number of switchers in the population has, in fact, probably been largely responsible for the increasing number of trade deals, as well as coupons, that have been offered by manufacturers in recent years.

Trade discounts can sometimes be effective in helping manufacturers gain or maintain distribution for a product. And although it is often considered negative that discounts can load the trade with product, increased inventories can help to ensure that the brand is never out of stock.

Price Buyers

Price buyers will often purchase a brand because it is on deal, provided that the special brings the price down to the level of that being charged for the least expensive competitive brands. Marketers who hope to generate volume from price buyers need to determine what price is currently being charged for other brands, and whether the retailer is likely to lower the price of the promoted brand to be competitive with the price leaders in the category.

Nonusers

Trade discounts are rarely effective at getting nonusers to try a brand in a category they don't use, since they don't give these people any reason to buy the product other than price.

Trade Promotions and Residual Value

Trade promotions are often seen as reducing the long-term value of brands. Consumers and retailers often use trade promotions as an opportunity to stock up on products, thereby reducing the number of purchases that they may need to make in the future. In addition, too-frequent trade deals can teach consumers and retailers to purchase only when a brand is being promoted and to reevaluate the amount that brand appears to be "worth."

Whether this actually occurs, however, depends on the type of product being promoted and how frequently the discounts occur. Occasional promotions for appropriate products can often attract retailer and consumer attention to a particular product, persuading them to buy it, thereby increasing the likelihood that it will continue to be successful in the long run.

Suppliers

Throughout this text we've suggested that you contact specialists and suppliers in various areas of sales promotion. We say that because it's almost impossible for one person to know all there is to know about every sales promotion technique. There is just too much information, and the risk is too great not to use every tool at your command. In addition, sales promotion is a very dynamic field—constantly changing and improving. You really need the best and most current advice you can get to make sure your sales promotion program works. That's why we suggest that you deal with the experts if you plan a promotion that requires specialized information.

To help you get started, on the following pages, we've listed some of the major sales promotion organizations and suppliers in various areas. This is not meant as a recommended list nor should it be considered a list of all the suppliers available. It is simply a list of companies and organizations who have long-term knowledge and experience in the field. In addition, most of them are members of the Promotion Marketing Association of America, Inc., the leading trade organization in the field.

You'll find listings for coupon redemption organizations, contest and sweepstakes suppliers, suppliers of continuity programs, fulfillment houses, sampling organizations, premium suppliers, and display and exhibit manufacturers. No doubt, you'll add others to this list as you become more involved in the field.

Coupon Redemption Organizations

American Premium Corp.
125 Walnut Street
Watertown, MA 02172
(617) 926-1800
(617) 923-1111

Donnelly Marketing
70 Seaview Ave.
Stanford, CT 06902
(203) 353-7000
(203) 353-7175 Fax

Johnstons & Assoc.
517 East Crosstown Pkwy.
Kalamazoo, MI 49001
(616) 345-0131
(616) 345-0189 Fax

Marketing Services Group/Creative Display Inc.
230 E. Ohio Street
Chicago, IL 60611
(312) 642-8212

NCH Promotional Services
1900 North Third Ave.
Clinton, IA 52733
(319) 242-4510
(319) 242-8343

H. Olsen & Co.
342 N. Fourth St.
Libertyville, IL 60048
(708) 362-0310

Carlson Marketing
P.O. Box 59159
Minneapolis, MN 55459-8208
(612) 540-5000
(612) 449-3888 Fax

Gage Fulfillment Group
1300 Highway 8
New Brighton, MN 55112
(612) 633-3700
(612) 633-5900

Stratmar Systems, Inc.
109 Willett Ave.
Port Chester, NY 10573
(914) 937-7171
(914) 937-0738 Fax

Contest and Sweepstakes Suppliers

Don Jagoda Assoc.
100 Marcus Drive
Melville, NY 11747
(516) 454-1800
(516) 454-1833

Marden-Kane, Inc.
410 Lakeville Road
Lake Success, NY 11042
(526) 326-3666

H. Olsen & Co.
342 North Fourth St.
Libertyville, IL 60048
(708) 362-0310

Promotion Marketing Corp. of America
90 Post Road West
Westport, CT 06880
(203) 227-8478
(203) 222-7690 Fax

Gage Fulfillment Group
1300 Highway 8
New Brighton, MN 55112
(612) 633-3700
(612) 633-5900 Fax

Ventura Associates
1350 Avenue of the Americas
New York, NY 10019
(212) 586-9720

Weston Group
320 Post Road W.
Westport, CT 06880
(203) 226-6933

Continuity Program Suppliers

Encyclopedia Britannica
310 South Michigan Ave.
Chicago, IL 60604
(312) 347-7000

Glendinning Companies
One Glendinning Place
Westport, CT 06880
(203) 226-4711
(203) 227-8121 Fax

Grosset and Dunlap
200 Madison Ave.
New York, NY 10016
(212) 951-8700
(212) 532-3693 Fax

Sunbeam Home Comfort
5224 N. Kedzie
Chicago, IL 60625
(312) 267-5100

Oneida Ltd.
Oneida, NY 13421
(315) 361-3211
(315) 829-3950 Fax

Samsonite Corp.
11200 E. 45th Avenue
Denver, CO 80239
(303) 373-2000
(303) 373-6000 Fax

Sperry & Hutchinson
315 Park Ave. S.
New York, NY 10010
(212) 598-3100

Sunbeam-Oster Housewares
8989 N. Deerwood Drive
Brown Deer, WI 58223
(414) 362-7120
(414) 362-7143 Fax

Fulfillment Organizations

D. L. Blair
1051 Franklin Blvd.
Garden City, NY 11530
(516) 746-3700
(516) 746-3889 Fax

John Blair & Co. (Shipply)
1290 Sixth Ave.
New York, NY 10104
(212) 603-5000
(212) 603-5453 Fax

Carlson Marketing Group
3825 W. Green Tree Rd.
Milwaukee, WI 53209
(414) 352-3450
(414) 351-7715 Fax

Marden-Kane, Inc.
410 Lakeville Rd.
Lake Success, NY 11042
(516) 326-3666
(516) 326-3679 Fax

Carlson Marketing Group
2280 Arbor Blvd.
Dayton, OH 45402
(513) 299-0700
(513) 299-9175 Fax

Carlson Marketing
P.O. Box 59159
Minneapolis, MN 55459-8208
(612) 540-5000
(612) 449-3888 Fax

Gage Fulfillment Book
1300 Highway 8
New Brighton, MN 55112
(612) 633-3700
(612) 633-5900 Fax

Stratmar Systems, Inc.
109 Willet Ave.
Port Chester, NY 10573
(914) 937-7171
(914) 937-0738 Fax

Weston Group
320 Post Road West
Westport, CT 06880
(203) 226-6933
(203) 454-2835 Fax

Sampling Organizations

John Blair & Co.
1290 Sixth Ave.
New York, NY 10104
(212) 980-5280
(212) 603-5453 Fax

Marketing Services Group/Creative Displays, Inc.
230 E. Ohio Street
Chicago, IL 60611
(312) 642-8212
(312) 642-7407 Fax

Donnelly Marketing
70 Seaview Ave.
Stamford, CT 06902
(203) 353-7000
(203) 353-7175 Fax

The Garber Co.
Union Street
Ashland, OH 44805
(419) 289-2666

Carlson Marketing
P.O. Box 59159
Minneapolis, MN 55459-8208
(612) 540-5000
(612) 449-3888 Fax

Gage Fulfillment Group
1300 Highway 8
New Brighton, MN 55112
(612) 633-3700
(612) 633-5900 Fax

Stratmar Systems
109 Willet Ave.
Port Chester, NY 10573
(914) 937-7171

Weston Group
320 Post Road W
Westport, CT 06880
(203) 226-6933

Premium Suppliers

American Premium Corp.
125 Walnut Street
Watertown, MA 02172
(617) 923-1111
(617) 923-8839 Fax

Anchor Hocking Corp.
1749 West Fair Ave.
Lancaster, OH 43130
(614) 687-2701
(614) 687-2079 Fax

Ansco Photo Optical
1801 Touhy Ave.
Elk Grove, IL 60007
(708) 593-7404

Bantam Books
666 Fifth Avenue
New York, NY 10019
(212) 765-7600
(212) 492-9862 Fax

Bic Pen
500 Bic Drive
Milford, CT 06460
(203) 783-2000
(203) 783-2081 Fax

Bulova Watch
1 Bulova Ave.
Woodside, NY 11377
(718) 204-3300

W. Atlee Burpee
300 Park Ave.
Warminster, PA 18974
(215) 674-4900
(215) 674-4170 Fax

Chase Packaging
53 Forest Ave.
Old Greenwich, CT 06870
(203) 637-5181

Corning Incorporated
Houghton Park
Corning, NY 14830
(607) 974-9000

Eastman Kodak
343 State Street
Rochester, NY 14650
(716) 724-4104
(716) 724-0663 Fax

Ecko Housewares
9234 W. Belmont Ave.
Franklin Park, IL 60131
(708) 678-8600

Fieldcrest/Cannon, Inc.
P.O. Box 27050
Greensboro, NC 27425
(919) 627-3000

Hamilton Beach Co./Proctor Silex
4421 Waterfront Dr.
Glen Allen, VA 23060
(804) 273-9777

Don Jagoda Associates
100 Marcus Drive
Melville, NY 11747
(516) 454-1800
(516) 454-1833 Fax

Carlson Marketing Group
3825 West Green Tree Rd.
Milwaukee, WI 53209
(414) 352-3450
(414) 351-7715 Fax

Libby Glass
940 Ash Street
Toledo, OH 43693
(419) 247-2387

Manhattan Shirt
1155 Avenue of the Americas
New York, NY 10036
(212) 221-7500
(212) 527-0695 Fax

Mattel Sales
5150 Rosecrans Avenue, M.S. 176
Hawthorne, CA 90250
(213) 524-2000
(213) 978-5913

Mirro/Foley
1512 Washington St.
Manitowoc, WI 54221
(414) 684-4421
(414) 684-1131 Fax

National Premium & Merchandising
2330 Commerce Drive
P.O. Box 247
New Berlin, WI 53151
(414) 782-1510
(414) 782-5878 Fax

Sunbeam Home Comfort
5224 N. Kedzie Ave.
Chicago, IL 60625
(312) 267-5100

H. Olsen & Co.
342 North Fourth St.
Libertyville, IL 60048
(708) 362-0310

Oneida, Ltd.
Oneida, NY 13421
(315) 361-3211
(315) 829-3950 Fax

RCA/Columbia Pictures Home Video
3500 W. Olive
Burbank, CA 91505
(818) 953-7900
(815) 953-7864 Fax

Rand McNally & Co.
8255 W. Central Park
Skokie, IL 60076
(708) 673-9100

Rawlings Sporting Goods
1859 Intertech Dr.
Fenton, MO 63026
(314) 349-3500
(314) 349-3588

Samsonite Corp.
11200 E. 45th Avenue
Denver, CO 80239
(303) 373-2000
(303) 373-6000 Fax

Simon & Schuster
1230 Avenue of the Americas
New York, NY 10020
(212) 698-7000
(212) 698-7007 Fax

Sony Corp.
9 West 57th Street
New York, NY 10019
(201) 930-1000
(201) 358-4060 Fax

Spaulding
257 Center Street
Garwood, NJ 07027
(908) 789-9229

Gage Fulfillment Group
1300 Highway 8
Minneapolis, MN 55112
(612) 633-3700
(612) 633-5900 Fax

Sunbeam-Oster Housewares
8989 N. Deerwood Drive
Brown Deer, WI 53223
(414) 362-7120
(414) 362-7143 Fax

Timex Corporation
P.O. Box 21126
Waterbury, CT 06720
(203) 573-5998
(203) 573-6901 Fax

Van Heusen
1290 Avenue of the Americas
New York, NY 10104
(212) 541-5200
(212) 247-5309 Fax

Van Schaack Premium Corp.
3600 S. Yosemite Suite 500
Denver, CO 80237
(303) 779-6000
(303) 773-3211

West Bend
400 Washington Street
West Bend, WI 53095
(414) 334-2311
(414) 334-6800 Fax

Weston Group
320 Post Road W.
Westport, CT 06880
(203) 226-6933

Whirlpool Corporation
2000 Administration Center, 63 North
Benton Harbor, MI 49022
(616) 926-3254
(616) 926-3568 Fax

Wilson Sporting Goods
2233 West Street
River Grove, IL 60171
(708) 456-6100

Display and Exhibit Manufacturers

Holl-Erickson, Inc.
8110 Ogden
Lyons, IL 60534
(708) 447-5540

Omnicom
50 S. Lively Blvd.
Elk Grove, IL 60007
(708) 981-0808

In-Store Programs

ActMedia, Inc.
30 Old Kings Highway South
Darien, CT 06820
(203) 655-2211
(203) 656-7122 Fax

ActNow, Aisle Vision, Carts, Impact,
Instant Coupon Machine, Shelf Take-One

Addvantage Media Group
7666 East 61st Street
Triad Center, Suite 600
Tulsa, OK 74133
(918) 254-6524
(918) 254-5071 Fax

Catalina Marketing
721 East Ball Road Suite 200
Anaheim, CA 92805
(714) 956-6600
(714) 956-5592 Fax

Checkout Channel
1 CNN Centre
Atlanta, GA 30303
(404) 827-4444
(404) 827-4434 Fax

Advanced Promotion Technologies
626 S. Military Trail
Deerfield Beach, FL 33442
(305) 425-7800
(305) 425-7837 Fax

Food World Games
1355 Terrell Mill Road Building 1476
Marietta, GA 30067
(404) 953-9691
(404) 951-2941 Fax

HMG Worldwide
475 10th Ave.
New York, NY 10018
(212) 736-2300
(212) 564-3395 Fax

In-Store Advertising
488 Madison
New York, NY 10022
(212) 593-9800
(212) 593-9198 Fax

MADD/Marketing Corporation of America
285 Riverside Ave.
Westport, CT 06880
(203) 222-1000

Marketing Force
1757 Northfield
Rochester Hills, MI 48307
(313) 853-6200
(313) 853-7909 Fax

Marketing Promotions
2814 New Spring Road Suite 103
Atlanta, GA 30339
(404) 333-9063
(404) 438-7589 Fax

Media One
150 East 58 St.
New York, NY 10022
(212) 755-7171
(212) 888-3866 Fax

Multimark Retail Field Services
2681 Parley's Way
Salt Lake City, UT 84109
(801) 466-2004

Stratmar Systems
109 Willet Ave.
PortChester, NY 10573
(914) 937-7171
(914) 937-6045

Supermarket Communications
148 East Ave. Suite 2I
Norfolk, CT 06851
(203) 852-0888
(203) 852-1277 Fax

VideoCart
300 S. Wacker Drive Suite 300
Chicago, IL 60606
(312) 987-5000
(312) 922-5096

Index

About the Authors

Don E. Schultz is Professor of Advertising and Integrated Marketing Communications at the Medill School of Journalism, Northwestern University, where he and his associates have pioneered the country's first graduate program in Integrated Marketing Communications. He is also President of his own marketing communications and management firm, Agora, Inc., and Director of the Promotion Marketing Association of America. Before joining Northwestern in 1977, Schultz was Senior Vice President of Tracey-Locke Advertising and Public Relations in Dallas. Schultz has authored five other books: *Sales Promotion Management, Integrated Marketing Communications, Strategic Advertising Campaigns, Essentials of Advertising Strategy,* and *Essentials of Newspaper Marketing.*

William A. Robinson is internationally recognized for his accomplishments in elevating the status of sales promotion as an integral part of the marketing mix. For more than 30 years, Chicago-based Robinson & Maites has helped Fortune 500 firms such as Procter & Gamble, AT&T, and McDonald's apply strategic, practical solutions to challenging marketing opportunities. Robinson appears frequently at marketing, sales promotion, and advertising workshops the world over. Robinson has authored three other books—*Sales Promotion Management, Promotional Marketing,* and *Best Sales Promotions.*

Lisa A. Petrison is a marketing consultant and adjunct professor at Northwestern University, where she teaches advertising and database marketing. She has held various professional positions in marketing, advertising, and public relations, and was a reporter for *Adweek* and *Promote* magazines. She has published articles on marketing and promotion in several professional and academic publications.

TITLES OF INTEREST IN MARKETING, DIRECT MARKETING, AND SALES PROMOTION

SUCCESSFUL DIRECT MARKETING METHODS, Fourth Edition, by Bob Stone

PROFITABLE DIRECT MARKETING, Second Edition, by Jim Kobs

CREATIVE STRATEGY IN DIRECT MARKETING, by Susan K. Jones

READINGS AND CASES IN DIRECT MARKETING, by Herb Brown and Bruce Buskirk

STRATEGIC DATABASE MARKETING, by Robert R. Jackson and Paul Wang

SUCCESSFUL TELEMARKETING, Second Edition, by Bob Stone and John Wyman

BUSINESS TO BUSINESS DIRECT MARKETING, by Robert Bly

INTEGRATED MARKETING COMMUNICATIONS, by Don E. Schultz, Stanley I. Tannenbaum, and Robert F. Lauterborn

NEW DIRECTIONS IN MARKETING, by Aubrey Wilson

GREEN MARKETING, by Jacquelyn Ottman

MARKETING CORPORATE IMAGE: THE COMPANY AS YOUR NUMBER ONE PRODUCT, by James R. Gregory with Jack G. Wiechmann

HOW TO CREATE SUCCESSFUL CATALOGS, by Maxwell Sroge

SALES PROMOTION ESSENTIALS, Second Edition, by Don E. Schultz, William A. Robinson and Lisa Petrison

PROMOTIONAL MARKETING: IDEAS AND TECHNIQUES FOR SUCCESS IN SALES PROMOTION, by William A. Robinson and Christine Hauri

BEST SALES PROMOTIONS, Sixth Edition, by William A. Robinson

INSIDE THE LEADING MAIL ORDER HOUSES, Third Edition, by Maxwell Sroge

NEW PRODUCT DEVELOPMENT, Second Edition, by George Gruenwald

NEW PRODUCT DEVELOPMENT CHECKLISTS, by George Gruenwald

CLASSIC FAILURES IN PRODUCT MARKETING, by Donald W. Hendon

THE COMPLETE TRAVEL MARKETING HANDBOOK, by Andrew Vladimir

HOW TO TURN CUSTOMER SERVICE INTO CUSTOMER SALES, by Bernard Katz

THE MARKETING PLAN, by Robert K. Skacel

ADVERTISING & MARKETING CHECKLISTS, by Ron Kaatz

SECRETS OF SUCCESSFUL DIRECT MAIL, by Richard V. Benson

U.S. DEPARTMENT OF COMMERCE GUIDE TO EXPORTING

HOW TO GET PEOPLE TO DO THINGS YOUR WAY, by J. Robert Parkinson

THE 1-DAY MARKETING PLAN, by Roman A. Hiebing, Jr. and Scott W. Cooper

HOW TO WRITE A SUCCESSFUL MARKETING PLAN, by Roman G. Hiebing, Jr. and Scott W. Cooper

DEVELOPING, IMPLEMENTING, AND MANAGING EFFECTIVE MARKETING PLANS, by Hal Goetsch

HOW TO EVALUATE AND IMPROVE YOUR MARKETING DEPARTMENT, by Keith Sparling and Gerard Earls

SELLING TO A SEGMENTED MARKET, by Chester A. Swenson

MARKET-ORIENTED PRICING, by Michael Morris and Gene Morris

STATE-OF-THE-ART MARKETING RESEARCH, by A.B. Blankenship and George E. Breen

WAS THERE A PEPSI GENERATION BEFORE PEPSI DISCOVERED IT?, by Stanley C. Hollander and Richard Germain

BUSINESS TO BUSINESS COMMUNICATIONS HANDBOOK, by Fred Messner

SALES LEADS: HOW TO CONVERT EVERY PROSPECT INTO A CUSTOMER, by Robert Donath, James Obermeyer, Carol Dixon and Richard Crocker

AMA MARKETING TOOLBOX (SERIES), by David Parmerlee & Allan Sutherlin

AMA COMPLETE GUIDE TO SMALL BUSINESS MARKETING, by Ken Cook

101 TIPS FOR MORE PROFITABLE CATALOGS, by Maxwell Sroge

HOW TO GET THE MOST OUT OF TRADE SHOWS, by Steve Miller

HOW TO GET THE MOST OUT OF SALES MEETINGS, by James Dance

MARKETING TO CHINA, by Xu Bai Yi

STRATEGIC MARKET PLANNING, by Robert J. Hamper and L. Sue Baugh

COMMONSENSE DIRECT MARKETING, Second Edition, by Drayton Bird

NTC'S DICTIONARY OF DIRECT MAIL AND MAILING LIST TERMINOLOGY AND TECHNIQUES, by Nat G. Bodian

For further information or a current catalog, write:

NTC Business Books
a division of *NTC Publishing Group*
4255 West Touhy Avenue
Lincolnwood, Illinois 60646-1975 U.S.A.